Best Seller

Sure Success in Interviews

Jayant Neogy

UNICORN BOOKS

Publisher
UNICORN BOOKS
F-2/16, Ansari Road, Daryaganj, New Delhi-110002
☎ 011-23275434, 23262683, 23250704 • *Fax:* 011-23257790
E-mail: info@unicornbooks.in • *Website:* www.unicornbooks.in

Branch : Mumbai
23-25, Zaoba Wadi, Thakurdwar, Mumbai-401002
☎ 022-22010941, 022-22053387
E-mail: rapidex@bom5.vsnl.net.in

Showroom :
★ **PM Publications,** New Delhi
- 10-B, Netaji Subhash Marg, Daryaganj
  New Delhi-110002
- 6686, Khari Baoli, Delhi-110006

ISBN 978-81-7806-046-0
Sure Success in Interviews

Edition: 2013

Printed at : Param Offsetters, Okhla, New Delhi-110020

Acknowledgement

It is not often that we get to fulfil a dream. Many years ago, as a fresh engineering graduate looking for a job and for career guidance, I had longed to get my hands on a not-too-expensive and no-nonsense guide on interview preparation. I could find none that I could afford, one that spoke to me as a friend and guide. Frustration! "Someday," I said to myself, "I will write my own useful and friendly guide for the fresher."

Earlier, when I had similar visions about writing a guidebook on resumes, I was lucky to receive enthusiastic support and valuable hints from my friends at Unicorn Books. As a result, *Winning Résumé* was written, published and did well at the bookstores.

Encouraged by this response, I have fulfilled the second part of my dream, writing a guidebook on interviews. I trust that the readers will find my *Sure Success in Interviews* as useful as *Winning Résumé*. Together, the two books form a complete career construction kit that will give you just the career boost that you need, whether you are just beginning your career or are already a veteran.

For helping me fulfil my dream, I thank the entire team at Unicorn Books, my patient wife and children and especially you, my dear readers, who inspired me to write *Sure Success in Interviews* by your wonderful response to *Winning Résumé*.

—Jayant Neogy
Palam Vihar, Gurgaon

Preface

Why Should You Buy This Book?

Let us face it. If you are a topper from an IIT or an IIM, you will probably not have to worry about your next interview or the lack of interview calls. Instead, you will be evaluating alternative job offers! However, for the vast majority of us, getting an interview call, or making sure that a job opportunity does not slip away, can be an all-consuming obsession in our lives at some time or the other. Our palms sweat, our throats run dry and our temples throb as the days go by and the pressure builds up!

As a result of this tension, when fickle opportunity does finally knock on our door, we are unprepared. Therefore, we are unable to give it our best shot. This is a great tragedy indeed!

It need not be so at all. Each one of us has knowledge, skills, aptitude, potential, ability and a burning desire to succeed. What we do not always have is the training and guidance to bring our qualities to the forefront, to package ourselves attractively and to make ourselves desirable in the eyes of the potential employer.

On the one hand, we need to acquire thorough and dispassionate knowledge about ourselves, our personal strengths and weaknesses. On the other hand, we need an understanding of the job's requirements. Then, we need the skill to match our strengths with the job requirements and offer the package to the potential employer with a degree of salesmanship that rarely comes naturally to us.

Sounds like an impossible task? Not at all! These are skills you can learn. What you need is commitment, perseverance and above all, good guidance. The very fact that you have picked up this book is a measure of your commitment and your willingness to work hard. What remains is good guidance.

That is what this book promises to give you – all the guidance that you need. On your part, you must promise to put in the toil and the sweat. Together, we will surely ace that interview!

What This Book Can Do For You

Doing well in the interview is all about preparation, practice, packaging and delivery. You prepare by knowing all about yourself. This book introduces you to the unique concept of a SWOT (Strengths, Weaknesses, Opportunities and Threats) analysis. You look at your own skills and accomplishments using the same powerful analytical tool that corporate management utilises to compete in the business world. You prepare by researching the company that has called you for the interview. In this book, you will get valuable tips on where to look for information and how to collect it.

After you have a clear understanding of your strengths and the company's needs, you practise your interview response skills. This book will provide you with tips for answering convincingly and to control your body language. As a result, you will be sincere, capable and enthusiastic – a winning combination.

The make-over section of this book is all about packaging yourself attractively. Here you will pick up valuable tips on how to dress correctly, groom yourself and carry yourself so that you appear a desirable addition to the staff of any organisation. You also learn how to prepare your professional and job portfolios that you will take with you to your interview.

Effective preparation, research, good dressing and grooming will all come together to inject confidence in your bearing. The practice sessions with the frequently asked questions will put you at ease in any interview situation and you will handle stress easily. You will know how to answer that tricky question, how to persuade the interviewer that you are the ideal candidate for the job and how to negotiate the salary to clinch the best deal for yourself.

The promise of this book is to make you a winner, one who will succeed in any interview.

What This Book Contains

For your comprehensive tutoring in interview success, it is best to read the book right through since all the chapters have something vital to say. However, we know that the needs will vary from reader to reader. With this in mind, the book has been structured so that you can go straight to the chapter that is relevant to you.

For instance, if your interview is tomorrow, you may wish to read Chapters 1 and 9, which work like a last-minute guide. On the other hand, if you are fresh to the job hunt, read Chapter 2, which is written specially for fresh graduates. If your interviews have gone well and you are already at the salary negotiation stage, read Chapter 8 for valuable tips on how to negotiate the best deal for yourself.

No matter what you need, this book has something useful for you! We give you a chapter-wise outline of what this book contains.

Chapter 1 - The Last-Minute Guide

Written especially for those who have little time left to prepare, we cover the key issues so that you can make the best use of the time you have available and, thereby, maximise your chances to ace that interview.

Chapter 2 - Especially for Fresh Graduates

This chapter is written for new entrants to the job market. We help you handle disappointments and show you how to turn things around. We discuss unconventional techniques to generate interview calls and tell you how to attack your career goals on a war footing.

Chapter 3 - Interviews Come in Different Flavours

Interviews can indeed be very different from one another. We discuss the main types and their characteristics in this chapter. Your strategy must be fine-tuned to the specific interview type that you are about to face. You learn the key feature of the campus interview, the walk-in interview and the telephone interview to understand the techniques needed to cope with each type.

Chapter 4 - Good Preparation is Half the Battle

Now we come to the nuts and bolts of preparation. This chapter tells you how to analyse your strengths and weaknesses using SWOT analysis, then to research the industry, the company and the job. Armed with these insights and knowledge, you match the job requirements to your accomplishments to create a winning combination. This chapter also tells you how to improve your body language and prepare yourself mentally so that your story is convincingly told.

Chapter 5 - Your Make-over & Portfolio

This chapter is all about dressing and grooming. We discuss appropriate interview attire for men and women. You learn the art of standing out from the crowd without appearing either too dowdy or too flamboyant. In this chapter, you are introduced to the concept of your professional and job portfolios. Portfolios guarantee that you will be noticed and appreciated in any interview.

Chapter 6 - The Big Moment is Here!

The big moment, for which you have prepared so hard, is here. This chapter takes you through all the stages of the interview, from the final preparations the day before to the opening moves, through the heart of the interactive session to the final closing stage when you ensure that the battle has been won and an offer will come your way. You learn what to ask when your turn comes and how to handle stress situations along the way.

Chapter 7 - Follow-up and Offer Evaluation

Your hunt for that job of a lifetime rarely ends with a handshake at the end of the interview. Much persuasion and perseverance is required since a top job does not fall in your lap like a ripe plum. The fine art of follow-up, the skill of turning a negative response into a positive one is discussed in this chapter. If you have multiple offers, this chapter helps you compare them and select the best.

Chapter 8 - Salary Negotiations

In this chapter you learn how to time salary negotiations to your advantage and how not to falter even if you are pressed to respond immediately to an offer. The importance of researching your market value before the negotiations is stressed. You will find a salary quiz to test your negotiation skills at the end of this chapter.

Chapter 9 - Frequently Asked Questions

In this invaluable chapter, you will find categorised questions you are most likely to encounter. In the section on difficult questions, an ordinary answer that most candidates give is compared with a top answer, with explanations for what makes it a top answer. The strategies you will learn and the confidence you get by practising with this question-answer section will go a long way in ensuring you succeed in any interview.

Chapter 10 - Pitfalls You Must Avoid

In this chapter, read about the reason why so many people fail in interviews. We look at the small but serious errors that many candidates commit so that you can avoid falling into a trap. We look at the means of handling weaknesses in your education and job history so that you can turn threats into opportunities.

Chapter 11 - A Bonus for You

We recognise that a great deal of success in shaping your career depends not just on the interview, but in making sure that you get interview calls from the right organisations. To help you win the battle of job hunting, we present you, as a special bonus in this chapter, an outline for writing and evaluating your own winning résumé.

Conventions Used in This Book

This book is designed for easy reading and quick reference. We have used attractive graphics to direct your attention to the tips, the pitfalls and the top answers that contain valuable insights.

Key thoughts are in bold text

Key points are highlighted throughout this book using bold text similar to the sample in this paragraph. While you skim through this book, you will be able to easily pick up valuable hints by merely reading the bold text.

TOP

A major part of any interview is in the form of questions and answers. Many questions are asked frequently in interviews and you can practise top answers for them. These answers are marked with a "thumbs up" sign, an icon of an upraised thumb.

Look for top answers in Chapter 9, *Frequently Asked Questions.* You will find top answers, similarly identified, in other parts of this book as well.

TIP

When important information exceeds a few lines and extends over an entire paragraph, a wise owl identifies the tip. You will find these tips distributed throughout this book, guiding you from one important tip to the next. Follow the owl and rapidly assimilate many good ideas.

And, finally:

TRAP

All endeavours have dangers and pitfalls. Preparing for your interview is no exception. It is easy to overlook something important or to give out a wrong signal or make untenable claims, which may be exposed later. Caution is called for. Traps are clearly identified in this book by the familiar skull and crossbones. Beware when you see this symbol and save yourself grief!

Best of luck in your job hunt!

Contents

1. The Last-Minute Guide

WHAT THIS CHAPTER CONTAINS

- Preparing for the interview
- Your image and body language
- Dressing for the interview
- Conducting yourself during the interview
- Closing the interview
- Salary negotiations

No! The boss does NOT have an eligible daughter! JLN

The Last Minute

If you are reading this chapter, the chances are your interview is tomorrow or the day after. You have no time for elaborate preparation, or for long practice sessions involving a comprehensive set of model questions and answers. You want practical hints and tips and you want them *now*. Time is running out!

Do not panic! In this chapter, we will give you just that, the essence of what will make you a better, more confident candidate. You will have to devote just two hours to the task. If you have more time, however, we urge you to read through the entire book, especially Chapter 9, *Frequently Asked Questions* and Chapter 10, *Pitfalls to Avoid.* An interview is too serious a matter to be taken via a shortcut!

Preliminary Thoughts

First, remember that only some interviewers, such as HRD professionals, really know how to hold interviews effectively. Most frontline interviewers that you will meet are managers and supervisors who have not been formally trained to take interviews. They are probably a little nervous too, just like you! Some do not even prepare in advance. Therefore, you can take control of the interview, and create a good impression, if you have prepared in the manner we describe in this chapter.

Only some interviewers are HRD professionals!

TIP

In many cases, regardless of the questions the interviewers may ask, what they really want to know is how well you will fit into the team. Whether you will reduce the team's workload or add to it. Therefore, when answering, be eager enough to show that you are a good team player and will pull your load, but not so eager as to be seen as a threat to the existing team members!

While it is important to impress people who may become your managers or supervisors, you may have to impress the company HRD representatives as well. You should expect very specific and personal questions from them, like your salary expectations. The HRD representatives are the ones who will conduct your reference checks. Therefore, they may well have the final say in your hiring.

Always research a company before your interview, and remember that attire, body language and manners count, in a big way. Try to avoid common mistakes. Try to show eagerness and interest in the job without appearing to be desperate.

Research the company before your interview

Remember, the interview is a two-way street. While the employer is judging you, you too are evaluating the employer. In fact, if you handle yourself well and ask the right questions, you may find that the interviewer is actually selling the merits of the job and the company to you. If this happens, you are really doing well!

Now let us look at this last-minute guide in more detail.

Interview Preparation

Begin Well

As in the case of a business meeting, sales call or any other important interaction with other people, the best way to succeed in an interview is to prepare well in advance and use the right strategy during the interview.

You must gather basic information such as the interviewer's name, its correct pronunciation, his or her position, company name and address. In addition, you should secure as much information as possible regarding the company's products or services, the market's perception of the company and the history of the company's growth and past performance. With this information, you will be well equipped to answer questions from a position of strength. This information will also assist you to evaluate the company as a potential employer.

As part of your preparation, it is also important that you prepare a list of questions to ask during the interview. As we have said earlier, do remember that the

A good interviewer will rate you high if you ask the right questions

interview is a two-way process. While the employer assesses your suitability for the job, you too must make sure that the company can provide you the environment and career opportunity you seek. A good interviewer will rate you highly if you ask pertinent and intelligent questions.

You should request information about the company and the job in advance. If possible, pick up the information yourself. Ask for annual reports, brochures, magazine or newspaper articles and the job description of the position advertised. These will not only help you prepare, but separate you from the others who do not ask for such information. Prepare your own questions and responses to anticipated questions. Practise until you are confident that you are as prepared as you can be. Ask for directions to where you are going and how long it will take to get there. Allow ample time for travel. Arrive five minutes early.

Some Tips for a Good Start

Here are some tips to help you prepare with facts and to ready your mind for the interview. The objective of the interview is to convince the interviewer that you are the most qualified and appropriate potential team member for them.

- Present a profile of yourself in less than two minutes. It is like a two-minute commercial.
- Show interest in the company, the job and especially the interviewer.
- Prove you are capable of performing rather than merely describing. Provide concrete examples that illustrate the successes you have achieved so far.
- Be positive, polite, and personable.
- Do not fabricate, guess or generalise, and do not get involved in a debate with the interviewer.

Understanding Yourself

To prepare well for the interview, begin by getting a full understanding of your own strengths and weaknesses, ambitions and employment requirements. This self-knowledge will make you a confident candidate, able to respond to questions without hesitation. Make sure that you have a well-prepared résumé covering personal details, education and qualifications, career history overview including employment dates, brief employer description, reporting structure, responsibilities, achievements and reason for leaving or wishing to leave your current job.

> ***Make sure you carry a well-prepared résumé with you***

Your Image and Body Language

The image you project to the interviewer during the interview is critical to your success. This image is conveyed unconsciously, by means of non-verbal body language. Even if you do not utter a single word, the way you look, sit, hold yourself and many other non-verbal clues will tell people a lot about you.

Interviewers make many subconscious decisions based on your image. These include your economic, social and educational level, your trustworthiness, level of sophistication, probability of success in the job and even moral character.

As a result, 90% of interviewers will form an opinion of you within the first minute of a preliminary meeting. In an interview, you will most probably be judged within the first four to five minutes.

Researchers have found that the impression you create is based 55% on the way you look (dressing and grooming), 38% on the way you physically behave (your body language) and only 7% on what you say. You can see, therefore, how vital it is to create a positive first impression! Your dress should reflect the culture of the company you are trying to enter. If in doubt, adopt a conservative,

> ***Your image depends 93% on how you look and behave and only 7% on what you say!***

corporate dress style such as a business suit for men and a sari ensemble for women.

Be sure that your grooming and hygiene are immaculate. Your posture, movements and mannerisms should be natural. Your manner of speaking should be clear and well enunciated so that you are clearly understood. Think of a newsreader on a professional television channel such as BBC or CNN. Convey the right amount of enthusiasm, sincerity, respect and warmth. Listen attentively and maintain good eye contact. Above all, organise your thoughts before you speak.

Your Basic Interview Strategy

It is important to be prepared for a variety of interview situations. Not all interviewers are skilled practitioners and you may experience considerable variations. However, you can develop a basic interview strategy. This will allow you to confidently adjust to any style of interview and ensure you are able to discuss your past performance, your relevant experience and your education and personal qualifications in an effective manner.

Here are some tips for formulating your basic interview response strategy:

- Mirror the style and pace of your interviewer. If the interviewer is friendly and chatty, try to be the same. On the other hand, if he or she is formal and uses quick-fire questions, respond in the same way.
- Do not anticipate questions and do not interrupt the interviewer.
- Maintain eye contact, but do not try to stare the interviewer down.
- Convey enthusiasm and warmth, but not the backslapping kind of friendliness.
- Use natural gestures and avoid nervous fidgeting.
- Ensure that you speak clearly.

You should feel relaxed and confident. After all, just as you need a job, the employer needs a good employee.

Dressing for the Interview

Interview Attire for Men

As we have already said, interviewers will make judgements about you within four to five minutes of an interview. If you appear clean, neat and polished, you will make a good impression.

Solid or pinstriped grey or navy-blue suit is always a good investment. However, if your budget does not allow you to buy a suit, you can wear a navy-blue shirt, with grey trousers and black shoes. If you are a fresh graduate and have your institute's blazer, it is a good combination with white shirt and grey trousers.

A conservative business suit is the best choice

Remember to wear a cotton vest or undershirt with your shirt even in hot weather, since it makes the shirt look whiter. Put on a shirt that is fresh from the cleaners just before the interview. Check your shirt to see if it needs pressing and keep your shoes freshly polished.

As for the tie, it should be of silk, striped, or have a small pattern such as dots. Avoid large, elaborate patterns or ties with too many colours.

Interview Attire for Women

Women will probably dress in a sari, salwar kameez or a business suit. With the sari, we suggest a white or ivory cotton blouse, with conservative neckline. Silk or polyester that looks like silk is a good choice too.

Choose silks in colder weather and cotton or polyester-cotton in warmer weather. Classic patterns in navy-blue, grey or some dark colour is generally the best. Lighter pastel shades are more common in summer. For certain jobs, especially for younger candidates, a dress may be preferred to a sari. Select a conservative dress with a jacket. However, the ensemble should not be too low cut, girlish or bright. On no account should you wear jeans to an interview!

We do not advise anyone to go for an interview in a short skirt unless you are looking for a position in the fashion industry. In traditionally male-dominated fields, such as banking and law, miniskirts and skirts with high slits are not advisable.

Remember that one's dress and grooming send out powerful messages to a prospective employer. Clinging clothes, purple or glittery fingernails, open-toe shoes and dangling earrings are inappropriate for an interview. Avoid loose or unruly hair. Pearl-stud earrings and a strand of pearls can add a touch of sophistication. The important thing is to wear just a few pieces of jewellery. Add one gold chain and a watch to your pearl set. Do not wear too many bangles or rings. They do not make you look efficient.

Your dress and grooming send out powerful messages to a prospective employer

Make sure that none of your nail polish is chipped and the colour is clear, pink or red. However, do not wear red to an interview at a financial institution or a conservative company.

Carrying a small briefcase is optional. Do not carry a casual shoulder bag or a shopping bag to an interview! Wear sandals with saris and pumps with dresses. If possible, select footwear that conceals toes. Lady's hats are virtually never seen in India—avoid them!

Arriving for the Interview

Normally you will have to wait for some time before you are called. Use that time to check out your grooming, and collect your thoughts. Be friendly to the receptionist. A light interaction will ease tension. If it is the company's policy to fill out an application, do so, even if you already have a résumé. The interviewer may need additional and specific information. Some organisations want everyone's history in the same format.

While you are waiting for the interviewer, do not pull out a novel from your briefcase. You should appear to be interested in business, current events or an industry publication, rather than some popular novel.

> ***Practise handshaking with your friends***

When the interviewer comes to greet you, smile broadly, shake his or her hand firmly and address him or her by his or her last name. Practise handshaking with your friends. It is important to avoid either a limp handshake, or a too hearty handshake. It may sound silly but a simple thing like a poor handshake can get the interview off to a bad start!

During the Interview

Often, the interviewer will begin by saying, "Tell me about yourself." It is best to answer this question after the job has been described to you so that you can tailor your response accordingly. If you have to talk first, describe yourself in two minutes or less and in a positive way. Say who you are and what you are interested in doing. Focus on the job's requirements and your accomplishments, highlighting wherever the two match.

Merely telling the interviewer that you are good at sales will not get you the job. You will be more effective if you can cite actual examples. Try to recollect your concrete achievements. Keep these memories handy so that you can recount them at the right time.

As you can see, you must have favourable facts and examples ready for use. You should actively seek opportunities to insert these self-advertisements during the interview. Responding at an interview is a skill that you acquire and improve upon as you attend more and more interviews.

Likely Questions

Here are some likely questions. Think of good answers to them. Your answers should be factual, quantified as far as possible and should hold you up in good light. If you think about the answers even the night before the interview, you will be able to find many telling points to score when the opportunity comes. Without this preparation, however, you will rarely think of top answers, complete with facts and figures, on the spur of the moment.

- Tell me about yourself?
- What are your goals? Short term and long term?
- What do you like doing the most?
- What are your strengths and weaknesses?
- How did you learn of our company?
- What do you know about the company?
- Why do you want to work for the company?
- Tell me about your previous job experience.
- Why did you leave your previous jobs?
- Why should we hire you?
- Why are you looking for another position?
- What have been your major achievements?
- Describe your ideal working environment.
- What type of management style do you work best with?
- What would your current manager say about you?
- In your most recent position, what have been your most significant accomplishments?
- What motivates you in the work environment?
- What frustrates you in the work environment?
- What would you bring to this position?
- How would you describe your own personality?

- What are some of your outside activities and interests?
- What are your strengths?
- What areas have you identified that you would like to improve on and what have you done about them?
- What are your career goals?
- What level of salary are you seeking?

This is far from a complete list. However, you should be able to put up a near professional performance if you go prepared to the interview with answers to these questions. If you have time, look at Chapter 9, *Frequently Asked Questions*, for more practice.

Typical Questions You May Ask

As we have said earlier, interviews have two-way traffic. While the interviewer is assessing you, you too should satisfy yourself that this is the right job for you. To help you decide, here are some questions you should ask during the interview.

- What is the reason for the vacancy?
- What are the key performance measures for this job?
- What are the company's growth plans?
- What are the company's latest sales and profits results?
- Who are the company's major competitors and what are the company's competitive strengths?
- Where does the company see itself going in the next three to five years?
- Where can this job lead to if I am a top performer?
- What education and training programmes does the company have?

Obviously, you need not ask all the questions listed here. The interviewer's response and body language to the first couple of queries will tell you whether you should ask more questions. Be warned that some companies are not very forthcoming. If you are encouraged to ask more about the job and the company, you have selected the right interview to appear in. If the answers are evasive, perhaps you will do better elsewhere!

> ***Watch the interviewer's response and body language before asking too many questions!***

Closing the Interview

Like a good beginning for the interview, a strong closing is equally important for your job prospects. If, at the end, you are really interested in the job, let the interviewer know this.

Ask the interviewer if you fit the requirements of the job. If you sense any reservation, you have an opportunity to overcome any of these objections right then and there. If you have done really well and the position is offered to you and you want it, accept it right away. If you want time to think it over, be courteous and tactful in asking for some time. Be sure to indicate a definite time frame in which you will respond.

The interviewer may need to communicate with others before a final decision can be taken. So, do not be discouraged if no definite offer is made or a specific salary discussed.

TIP

Should you feel the interview is not going well, do not let your discouragement show. It is possible that your reactions are being tested. Always thank the interviewer for his time and the consideration shown to you. As you arrived with a smile, remember to depart with a smile as well.

Salary Negotiations

Most companies have a salary range for each job. The range offered to you will depend on your qualifications and experience. You cannot change this, but you can bargain shrewdly within the range. Your bargaining ability will depend on how well you have researched the going market rate for the job and your own market value. You must, of course, do this research in advance.

> ***Your bargaining ability will depend on the quality of your prior market research***

Even with limited time, phone calls to friends and relatives working in the same industry will give you some broad indicators of what you can expect. In addition, you may wish to sharpen your bargaining skills by using some of the tactics we describe below.

If the interviewer asks you pointed questions like:

- Have you thought about salary?
- What salary are you expecting?
- What is the minimum salary you would accept?

You can turn the situation around and put the ball back in the interviewer's court by answering the question with a question. For example, you may ask:

TOP

- What is the salary range for this position?
- My current salary is X. What is your authorised salary range for the job?
- Most of my peers, who are also business management graduates, have been receiving offers in the Rs 2 to 3 lakh per annum range. What is the authorised salary range for this position?

If you have time left, do read Chapter 9, *Frequently Asked Questions* and Chapter 10, *Pitfalls to Avoid.* They may prove invaluable for your interview. Good luck!

2. Especially for Fresh Graduates

WHAT THIS CHAPTER CONTAINS

- Handling and reversing application rejections
- Applying Napoleon's strategy to the job hunt
- Three effective job-hunt techniques
- Job hunt on a war footing

We ARE looking for young blood, but this is ridiculous!

JLN

Especially for Fresh Graduates

In this chapter, we look at the special problems of fresh graduates still waiting for a job offer. Indeed, instead of offers, a number of rejections may have undermined your confidence. You realise that what you have been doing so far, though done with a great deal of sincerity, is not good enough. If this description fits you, then it is time to change your game plan.

First, we will tackle the rejections. Given below are some novel tips and techniques that you can use to turn the rejections around and create opportunities where you see only a blank wall. Later in this chapter, we will show you how you can raise your efforts to a higher level using tips and techniques that are both unusual and effective. You may find some of the ideas new and unfamiliar. However, if you apply them with determination and persistence, they will work for you.

Turning rejections into opportunities

Handling Rejection

Whether the rejection slip comes by mail, phone, or fax, the message always seems the same and your heart turns cold and your spirits droop. Do not despair! All of us get knocked down in life from time to time. What really matters in the long run is whether you can get up again and fight! When you feel that you have reached the end of the road and there is no ray of hope in the darkness, use some of the techniques explained below to bounce right back!

The Rejection Reversal Technique

Rejection can be difficult to bear, especially when it comes from the employer you were most interested in. However, you can use this setback as an opportunity to grow, learn, and possibly reverse the rejection.

Do not hesitate. Immediately call the person who wrote the letter to request feedback: "Why do you think I did not meet your needs? What do I lack?" Listen closely to the reply. If you are provided with a valid

Call back immediately to get feedback

reason why you did not meet the job's needs, take note of it and politely thank the manager for taking time to speak with you. However, if the answer indicates that some information was misunderstood, or you failed to provide some required information, then you can take the opportunity for turning the situation around. Follow up to furnish the missing information or correct any misunderstanding that might have occurred and you may just persuade the employer to rethink.

If the employer gives you a valid reason for unsuitability, at the very least, you will come to know of some correctable shortcoming in you that you can take care of well before the next interview.

The Isolation Technique

If you are not sure whether you are getting the real reason from the employer for your rejection, you can use specific questions to dig a little deeper and try to isolate the real cause. For instance, you may be told that your salary expectation was too high. You offer to lower your expectations. But at that stage you are told that the employer was also looking for more experience. While this discussion will probably not get you the job, you will at least be reassured that your salary demand was not unrealistic. Your market value is reconfirmed and the rejection does not appear so demoralising after all.

Dig deeper to uncover the real reason

The Second Wave Technique

Perhaps you were rejected at a preliminary stage, say at a campus interview. Generally, someone from the employer's personnel department may have come to the campus for the preliminary sorting. If you believe that you possess the requisite qualifications and you should be seriously considered for the job, then commit yourself to turning the situation around and getting another interview.

You create this 'second wave', this appeal for a second interview, by contacting the manager who would have been your boss if you had got the job. If your background is highly specialised (say, an accountant or engineer), you can rightfully explain that you were unable to demonstrate your technical expertise as you were speaking with a personnel department person. Point out that you think you can do a better job of conveying your expertise if you were interacting with a fellow professional like your possible boss. You will be surprised how often the 'fellow professional against personnel' appeal works. If you play your cards right, there is a very good chance that you will succeed in getting a second interview. The second wave may carry you to fortune!

The 'fellow professional against personnel' approach

The Persistent Suitor Technique

One of the more difficult situations in a job search is to deal with a less-than-enthusiastic personnel department. You can get caught in the waiting game, hoping for the phone to ring. The job search is your number one priority, but it may be far down the list for the personnel department. For instance, they may be in the middle of negotiating a new contract with their staff union. In that case, your application may be shelved for a long time. During the resulting long wait with no response, most job seekers will simply give up. Do not include yourself among these quick quitters. Keep in touch and continue to follow up.

You may find yourself calling every week only to hear a "nothing has changed" response. Be patient but persistent. Continue your efforts to move the process forward. You use this technique like the proverbial persistent suitor, who will not take 'no' for an answer. Remember that the 'No' on a rejection letter does not always mean 'no'. Sometimes, it simply means "not yet".

Taking the Fight to the Enemy

Having successfully kept your spirits up in spite of a few rejections, it is now time to take the offensive. We will devote the rest of this chapter to explore some aggressive but effective techniques to reach your goal, which is a good job for you! We begin our campaign by adopting Napoleon's strategy.

Napoleon's Strategy

The techniques in this chapter will create opportunities for you where you thought none existed! However, a great deal of hard work will have to be put in by you. Believe me! This is not the time to take a vacation or to take time off from the job hunt. Instead, it is time for you to actually double your efforts and create your own opportunities. You have to think like the man who said: "If opportunity does not knock, I will build a new door!"

> ***If opportunity does not knock, build a new door!***

You have to try much harder since you are one of the thousands flooding the job market. However, there is one major difference. You, amongst all others, have decided to fight back. You have bought this book! As you read this chapter, your resolve will be reinforced by many new tricks and techniques that you will learn, perhaps for the first time. For instance, you will learn how to use Napoleon's strategy, which is to keep pushing at the enemy's battle lines until you see a vulnerable point. Then you apply all your might and energy to penetrate through that weak point you have just found.

If you have not already done so, go back and read this book from cover to cover. You will find several keys that can unlock closed doors and uncover new pathways. You have to keep trying. Your watchword will be "I will never, ever give up!" To tackle your immediate problem, that of getting a job offer, concentrate on the tips and techniques that will be revealed to you now.

General Techniques

Here are three general techniques that will get you back on track on your job hunt. Later in this chapter we will look at some special techniques that you may have to use as well.

Networking

Contact all your friends and classmates who have just graduated. If they have found a job, congratulate them. Then ask if there were any offers that they had turned down during the course of their own job search. If the position and company happen to be in your field, ask your friend for the company's contact information and his personal recommendation. The employer may not have filled the position yet, and the recommendation from a candidate they had chosen earlier, may provide you with an immediate opportunity for being considered for that vacancy.

> ***Follow up on any job offers that a friend may have turned down***

The Retracing Technique

If you are without a job offer, and six months or so have passed after graduation, the first thing you should do is to retrace your job search steps over the past six months. Begin by contacting one by one, all the employers who had interviewed you. Do not leave out any employer.

> ***Call up every employer who has interviewed you and let them know you are still available***

There are several good reasons for doing this. The first reason is that many employers have a last minute drop out. This may be because the selected candidate got a better offer, decided to study further or was selected in a competitive examination such as the IAS. Few companies want to begin the hiring process all over again. In larger companies there are usually a fixed number of fresh positions to be filled, such as management trainees. In such a case, you may get hired because you are the right person at the right time!

The second reason why follow-up is a good idea is that even if you are told "Sorry, nothing is available", you have the opportunity to demonstrate your eagerness and sincerity. If you get another opportunity for an interview later, your interest and persistence will speak well for you.

TIP

If you are uncomfortable about how to reopen the dialogue, say that you wish to update the employer's database with your address and phone number just to be sure that they have no difficulty if they wish to contact you. If your address or phone number has changed, then you have a very valid reason for making the call!

Intensive Job Search

Draw up a timetable for carrying out a job search. Make sure that you are devoting enough time to locate new employment opportunities. Identify potential employers using all the contacts you have amongst friends, relatives, your institute's alumni association and the teachers in your institute.

Once you have created a list of probable employers, you can start contacting them to find out if they have any opening for you. It is important not to be inhibited by the feeling that your jobless state is a stigma on your abilities. The market may be in recession, there may be political uncertainties or the fear of war. All this may slow the process of getting a job. However, your hard work and persistence will surely pay off in the end.

> ***Your jobless state is not a stigma!***

Special Techniques

The Offer-You-Cannot-Refuse Technique

What should you do when an employer says, "I'm sorry, we do not have any job openings"? Do you just give up? Cross them off your list? If you do, you are overlooking a large segment of the 'hidden job market' that we hear so much about. By utilising a common sales technique that we will describe below, you can tap into this potentially significant source of employment.

The technique we now examine is based on the core assumption that if you cannot get into a desirable organisation in any other way, it is still a good long-term investment for you to offer your services to them at a reduced cost on a temporary or part-time basis. If the employer is indeed reputed and you foresee vacancies in the near future, it is a good strategy to join them as a volunteer, even without salary if required. Few employers will be able to resist the opportunity to get qualified help at low cost or no cost. They are bound to be impressed by your genuine desire to work for them and your persistence.

If and when vacancies arise, you will be ahead of any competition since you will be there and you will already know the people and the job quite well. Even if no opening materialises, your temporary or voluntary work experience will only strengthen your next job application.

This technique will not always work but it does give you a unique approach that few others will think of. If you turn in an outstanding performance, you stand an excellent chance of filling in a vacancy when one arises.

TRAP

Be warned that this technique is not for everybody, nor for all organisations. You will have to use your judgement whether it is appropriate to use it. Make sure that you are comfortable with the idea of working sincerely and hard as a volunteer. Thereafter, check if the employer will react favourably.

In general, a young and progressive company, such as an Information Technology start-up company, is more likely to respond favourably to this technique, rather than an old, established and conservative organisation.

The Freelancer Technique

The Freelancer Technique works especially well in those fields where freelancing (independent contracting) is commonplace, as in the advertising field. Put together a full portfolio of your work samples and a write-up on the services you can provide. Speak to a few small-to-medium advertising firms who appear to have full order books. The services you can offer may include freelance writing, design, and voice dubbing for commercials. Try to approach the owner or creative director of the agency. Write letters to these individuals, introducing yourself as a freelancer. Follow up the letters a week later with phone calls and set up appointments with those who sound interested. Now you have the chance to show your work portfolio and open the door when future needs arise. Follow up with a thank-you note.

Do not be surprised if in a few months' time you are converted from a totally unknown person to the best-known freelancer in the business! You will get freelance contracts and one of your clients may eventually employ you full time if you do your work well.

Although the example here is from advertising, this technique works equally well in all areas where independent contracting is common, for instance, in creative fields (Advertising, Publishing, Writing, Arts), technical fields (Programming, Engineering), and specialty fields (Accounting, Legal, Medical). The earnings are usually quite good and may actually be 25% higher than regular wages! You will, of course, get no perquisites or retirement benefits.

Freelancing will work in advertising, publishing, programming, accounting and many other fields.

TIP

It usually costs very little to establish yourself as a freelancer. You have to put together your work portfolio and outline your services. However, you can often work from your home, so that you require no office establishment costs.

3. Interviews Come in Different Flavours

WHAT THIS CHAPTER CONTAINS

- Different types of interviews and how to handle them
- The trusted trio of application, interview and reference check
- Supplementary tests such as the stress test
- Tips for handling campus interviews and walk-in interviews

No! Your dog cannot be one of your references!

JLN

Interviews Come in Different Flavours

Before you get down to the nuts and bolts of preparing for your interview, you need a clear idea of the type of interview you are preparing for. We look at the different types of interviews and the best way to prepare for each.

The Most Common Type of Interview

In most types of interviews, you will have to go through a selection process, which is called 'sieving'. The objective of the process is to gradually eliminate candidates by weeding out the least eligible until the number of candidates that remain match the number of vacancies available. The interview is just one of the sieving stages in the selection process. The entire set of steps may be listed as follows:

Advertisement
↓
Applicants → Reject
↓
Consider Further
↓
References → Reject
↓
Consider Further
↓
Interview → Reject
↓
Final Selection

This process depends on the classic trio consisting of:

1. Application Form
2. Letters of Reference
3. Interview

While there are other methods of selection, an overwhelming majority (varying from 82 to 96%) depend on just these three procedures in sequence. Sometimes, the references may be checked after the interview, instead of before.

Verification of Supplied Information

Potential employers will verify information such as academic qualifications and current salary drawn. Therefore, you should be very sure of what you put down in your application as you may be required to substantiate what you have written.

You do have some freedom regarding information you give on the reasons for wanting to leave the current employment, wanting to join the prospective employer and on hobbies or extra-curricular activities.

TIP

However, do not be too "creative". Remain low key if the facts are not very helpful to your cause. On the other hand, do not miss an opportunity to highlight any favourable point in your application and substantiate it with proof at the interview.

Supplementary Tests

In addition to the Classic Trio of Application Form, References and the Interview, some organisations use additional tests for selection. The three most common tests are:

- Psychological Tests
- Group Exercises/Discussions
- Stress Interviews

These are only supplementary tests. The key factors that decide your selection are still the information in your application, the response by your referees and, of course, the outcome of your interview.

Psychological Tests

Psychological tests go back to the early 20th century when Alfred Binet devised intelligent tests for children. A popular adult test for intelligence in the US is the Army Alpha Test, later modified as the National Intelligence Test for civilian use. Today, many multinational and Indian companies use similar tests to supplement interviews.

TIP

Prepare for such tests by calming yourself. Do not over-react to questions thrown at you deliberately to induce stress. You have little to worry from such tests if you are well prepared and in control of yourself.

Group Exercises/Discussions

Group exercises are usually used for identifying candidates with leadership potential. They are used to deal with a large number of candidates at one time. They are typically used at army recruitment centres and in campus interviews. Group exercises often involve a leaderless group discussion assigned to solve a given problem. Observers note the dynamics of the group, the way candidates interact and whether natural leaders emerge during the exercise.

Prepare for group discussions if you are facing an admission test into a management college, a campus interview or seeking recruitment through a competitive examination. For thorough training in this particular form of testing, you may consider joining a specialised study circle to practise group discussions and group exercises.

Stress Interviews

In a stress interview, the interviewer(s) will try to test how you react under pressure by firing rapid questions at you, or deliberately being aggressive or offensive. The purpose is to see how you handle yourself under stress. The interviewer may be sarcastic or argumentative, or may keep you waiting.

The best way to deal with such a situation is to be mentally prepared for something like this to happen so that you are not taken by surprise. If you

TIP

do face a stressful situation in an interview, do not take it personally. Calmly answer each question as it comes. Ask for clarification if you need it and never rush into an answer.

The interviewer may lapse into silence at some point during the questioning. Recognise this as an attempt to unnerve you. Sit silently until the interviewer resumes the questions. If a minute goes by, ask if he or she needs clarification about your last comment. In short, play it cool!

Some Special Types of Interviews

Most of the time, the interviews you face will follow the lines we have just described. Typically, they will be held in the organisation's office. However, there are special types of interviews that are becoming quite common in India.

Let us look at:

- Campus Interviews
- Walk-in Interviews
- Telephone Interviews

Campus Interview

In a typical campus interview, you will spend 20 to 30 minutes in a tiny cubicle with a total stranger. This person will subsequently decide whether you will ever have a chance of working for their company. The best you can hope for is to avoid being disqualified, which only takes you one step further into the interviewing maze. One little mistake, one little error, and you could be history!

Actually, the entire process seems rather absurd, except for the fact that you will not get a job without playing the interviewing game and campus interviews are often the starting point for the hiring process.

A campus interview is not simply meeting with five or even ten companies and then picking the one you want to work for. To maximise

> *It is not enough to show up. You have to perform at peak in each campus interview*

chances of your success, you have to first maximise the number of your interviews, and then maximise your interview efficiency. It is not enough to just show up for the interviews, you have to perform at your peak in each encounter.

The Company's Interviewing Process

Most hiring companies go through four distinct steps in their campus hiring process:

Marketing – popularising the company's name on campus

Screening – weeding out candidates who do not meet the company's basic criteria

Assessing – a candidate's behaviour against the company's approved behaviour profile

Selling – encouraging the chosen candidates to choose the company as an employer.

The first two steps will take place on campus. The final two will follow at the company's office or factory. Your objective is to reach the fourth step, where you will be courted as the employee the company wants. But before you get there, you must succeed in the campus interview.

Here are some hints and pointers to help you. Remember, however, that for assured success, you must read and use the knowledge contained in the entire book and not just these tips!

Know Your Competition

Right now, they are sitting there in class with you. They will also be sitting there in the interview waiting room or shaking hands with the interviewer either before or after you. All those students you have been competing with for marks and rank are now your direct competitors for jobs that are being offered at your campus. It appears to be an annual examination all over again. But there is one important difference now.

This time, it is not how much you know, but how well you communicate that will matter.

> ***In campus interviews, it is not how much you know, but how well you communicate that matters***

Know your competition and what they have to offer. Know yourself and what you have to offer. Be ready to differentiate and sell your own candidature based upon your unique set of skills.

How to Choose the Very Best Companies

Choose your preferred companies wisely. Year after year, students flock to the household-name companies that come to campus (Hindustan Lever, Larsen & Toubro, a Tata company and so on), while some of the best employers go almost unnoticed, unable to fill their interview calendar because they are not well-known. Only few knowledgeable students do the research needed to find out the best performers. Indeed, many of the smaller companies are more growth-oriented and offer better opportunities for career advancement than the blue chips.

At the all-important beginning of your career, do your research in advance and choose wisely. Do not get carried away by the blue-chip tag that some companies carry. Just as you would find out all the critical facts about a company before you buy their shares or invest money in them, you owe it to yourself to research any potential employer before the campus interviews begin.

> ***Research the potential employers thoroughly***

Invitational Interviews

Some organisations practise the invitational interview or "closed" interview. In a closed interview, your institute forwards the résumés of all interested students to the employer. Before the campus visit, the employer selects those who will be called for the interview.

The key here is to tailor each and every résumé you submit to suit the targeted employer. Do not try to save time or effort by handing out copies of an all-purpose résumé. It is much better to take an extra half-

TIP

hour to write your résumé specifically for a particular employer than to miss being called by him because your application was insipid.

Ask the Career Placement Office in your institute at the beginning of the semester for names of companies who will hold closed interviews. Then ask for as much information as possible about each of these employers and their job requirements, including any minimum requirements such as cut-off percentages, class obtained or major subject combinations. Prepare your résumé to emphasise those aspects of your background that meet or exceed the employer's requirements.

Emphasise the positives in your background that match the needs of a particular employer. Then submit your personalised résumé to the Career Placement Office for despatch to each employer. While you may keep a generic résumé with the Placement Officer for use at short notice, use a personalised résumé as far as possible.

Timing is Everything

Always request the last or second-to-last interview slot of the day. These are the interviews that the interviewer will remember best at the end of the day. Therefore, if you want to be remembered, make it as late in the day as possible.

What to Take Along

In addition to yourself, take your 9"×12" portfolio/folder, two copies of your résumé, copies of your top three letters of recommendation and any company information you have gathered. Read the section on Portfolio Preparation in Chapter 5, *Your Make-over and Portfolio*, for details of what your portfolio should contain. You should be well rehearsed for a 'two-minute commercial' about yourself, describing why you are a star candidate for the company interviewing you.

Impress the Interviewer

If you have done a good job of researching the company, carry the company information such as annual reports and brochures in plain view, where it can be easily seen, and not inside your portfolio or folder. You want the recruiter to know that you have done your homework.

Visit your Career Placement Office in advance. If the interviewing company has visited your campus before, it is quite likely that the office has a folder containing brochures and annual reports. If you cannot carry away the original, get the material photocopied. Do not worry if the information is six months or a year out of date. You can ask the recruiter for an update. Now you will surely be noticed!

TIP

Make sure you know the company information inside and out. Be ready and willing to demonstrate your understanding of the company when asked. If you do it well, you will surely impress the campus interviewer.

Acing Your Interview

Near the end of your campus interview, you will be given an opportunity to ask questions. Say something along these lines: "From everything I have heard today, combined with my research about your company, I am very interested in going on to the next step. Please let me know, are you interested in me?"

If you get even a mildly encouraging response, ask your final question: "What is our next step?" Take careful note of the actions that need to be taken. This is what you must do to get that vital second interview.

TIP

Leave an excellent final impression by writing out your 'thank you' note and handing it just before the interviewer leaves at the end of the day. Keep some attractively printed 'thank you' cards with you for this purpose.

By taking these simple steps, you will definitely stand out from the crowd.

Walk-in Interviews

Walk-in interviews are becoming quite common these days as a means of entry-level recruitment. Organisations can attract a large number of local candidates to such interviews with minimum effort. The candidates too like interviews where no application forms have to be filled in advance.

> ***Based on appearance and first impressions, candidates are evaluated quickly in walk-in interviews***

As in any type of interview, unless you do your homework, you will end up wasting your time at a walk-in interview. These interviews have a set of rules and protocols all their own. For instance, they are designed to process a very large number of applicants in a very short time. Therefore, employers evaluate candidates quickly, based on appearances and first impressions. You must know the correct techniques to create the right impression in the short exposure time that you will get as a candidate. Otherwise, you will not succeed in walk-in interviews.

TIP

Usually a full 50% or more of the candidates at walk-in interviews are window shoppers. They are not serious. Often, they are just browsing to see what is available in the marketplace. In order to stand out amongst so many not-so-serious candidates, you require a fairly aggressive and well-planned approach.

Types of Walk-in Interviews

There are three basic types of walk-in interviews that you may encounter. Watch and listen carefully from the side so that you can determine the interview type and adjust your approach accordingly. Here are the three basic types:

Screening Interview

This interview lasts no more than two to three minutes and is usually conducted by companies that are mainly interested in gathering résumé and initial impressions. Your strategy should be to quickly point out the key areas in your résumé that match the job's requirements. Pay close attention to the questions being asked to candidates who are interviewed before you so that you can note the job requirements and match them with your areas of strength. You should position yourself in the line so that you can overhear at least two or three interviews before your turn comes.

Mini-Interview

These interviews usually last five to ten minutes and are conducted in a cabin. Be prepared to give full details of your background and highlight your strengths in relation to the job requirements. At this stage, you must be prepared to elaborate and explain all items that are covered in your résumé, relating to qualifications, experience etc. Ask the interviewer for a business card and inquire what the next step will be.

Full Interview

The full interview usually takes place behind a curtain or screen at the employer's cabin, or it may be arranged in another part of the hall. In most cases, you will be invited to the full interview only after being accepted at the previous screening interview or mini-interview. Be prepared to spend 20 minutes or more, but probably no longer than 30 minutes, since most companies have a tight schedule to keep. If the job is technical, you may be interviewed by technical or line managers at this stage. This interview is like any full-scale interview and your preparation will have to be comprehensive.

At the end of the interview, if you are truly interested, let the interviewer know of your interest and ask what the next step will be. Assume that the company is also interested in you.

Your Interviewers

You will usually meet Personnel or Human Resources recruiters at preliminary walk-in interviews. They make their living as professional screeners. Their job is to weed out the undesirables so that hiring managers, who conduct the full interviews, can spend more time with the candidates they are truly interested in.

TIP

Your strategy for the first two interview stages is to avoid elimination. You have to convince the interviewer that you meet or exceed the minimum requirements of the job. It is also important to quickly form a rapport with the interviewer since he is going to form a yes or no opinion of you in a short time.

Observe the interviewer carefully. If he stands in front of the desk, he is likely to be informal and not too technical. Try to respond in an easy, confident and informal manner. Your poise, body language and communication skills will matter more than your mastery of facts. Keep your answers short. Do not elaborate with too much data.

Adjust your response to suit the interviewer's style

If, on the other hand, the interviewer sits behind the desk, taking notes and looking serious, expect probing and technical questions. Concentrate on facts and figures to support your candidature rather than poise and style.

Your Portfolio

As with all interviews, you must be thoroughly prepared for a walk-in interview. Bring at least two copies of your résumé. If your standard résumé does not have all your key selling points on the first page, it should be reworked. In a walk-in interview, impressions are formed quickly and decisions are taken fast. There is very little chance that the interviewer will ever see any vital information about you if you put it on page 3!

Put all vital information on page one of your portfolio

You will not need a covering letter since you will hand over the résumé personally. If there is any vital information in your covering letter, such as your contact telephone number, make sure you include this information on the very first page of your revised résumé for the walk-in interview.

You should have copies of the top three letters of recommendation that you have obtained in advance, before the interview.

Store all your documents in a leather or vinyl-bound portfolio. Include a small notebook, a pen and a few personal visiting cards. If you have a slim and presentable briefcase, use it; otherwise, invest in a new portfolio folder. For more details on portfolios, see Chapter 5, *Your Make-over and Portfolio*, later in this book.

Your image is crucial at a walk-in interview, perhaps even more important than at a normal interview, since decisions are made much more quickly. This is not the time to model the latest in campus fashions, however. Make sure you wear a classic business suit or a blazer and tie with grey trousers. Keep your dress and appearance conservative so that the interviewer focuses on you, not your clothes. You will get much more information on dressing and grooming in Chapter 5, *Your Make-over and Portfolio*.

In a walk-in interview, your image is even more crucial than in a normal interview!

On-the-spot Preparation

In this book, Chapter 4, *Good Preparation is Half the Battle*, is devoted entirely to the preparation before an interview. However, walk-in interviews require special treatment. Normal methods are not very effective, since you have very little time to prepare. Very often, you are responding to a newspaper advertisement seen in the morning for a walk-in interview scheduled to start within hours.

TIP

Here is what you do. Instead of just getting into line, approach the interviewer's table from the side and quietly pick up some of the publicity literature that is usually displayed on the table. Then take a few steps back. By staying four to six feet away and listening, you will be far enough to be unobtrusive, yet still within earshot of any conversation that is taking place. Listen to what the recruiter asks. Be prepared to answer the same questions yourself. Listen to the responses. Did the recruiter respond positively or negatively? Listen to two or three different interviews to compare different responses. If there is more than one recruiter for the company, note the different styles of each and choose the one who fits your own personality type.

What you have accomplished so far is considerable. You have in hand some information about the company, its past performance, its future plans and its thrust areas. You have some idea of the type of questions being asked and the interviewer's response to different types of answers. If there is more than one recruiting cabin, you have a feel of which interviewer suits your own style. This is far more information than what any candidate has in a normal closed-door, sit-down interview!

TOP

Congratulations! You have just taken a simple step that will put you really far ahead of your competitors. When your turn arrives, step up with confidence, introduce yourself, and state clearly why you fit the needs of the recruiter like no one else. You will truly stand apart from the crowd.

You may feel a bit uncomfortable with this technique at first because your natural tendency is to get in the line. However, walk-in interviews do require an unconventional approach.

Follow-up

To create a lasting impression and successfully follow up on your walk-in interview, you can adopt similar techniques as in campus interviews. Read the section on campus interviews, earlier in this chapter, for more details on follow-up.

The Telephone Interview

Many employers today telephone candidates after receiving their job applications. While the call may be just to fix an appointment, in some cases, a preliminary evaluation is done over the phone. In today's competitive world, how you respond to a phone call from a potential employer may well decide whether you get an interview call from them or not. Therefore, such calls have to be treated with the respect they deserve. Here is how to handle phone interviews successfully.

Read about the preparation for phone interviews and study the helpful tips given below to ensure that each call from a potential employer is fully exploited by you.

Preparation

Phone interview calls may come unexpectedly. Yet, you can be prepared for them. Here are some of the things that you should do in anticipation:

- Tape your résumé to a wall in full view of the phone. It will be there if and when you get a phone interview call. If you are looking for a job, the résumé is a constant reminder to you to keep on with your job search.
- Keep all company research materials within easy reach of the phone. Use a folder with tabbed separators so that you can quickly locate the material you need.
- Have a notepad and pen handy for notes.

Some Helpful Tips

Anticipate the dialogue you are likely to have. Write a general script with answers to questions that you might be asked. Focus on your skills, experiences, and accomplishments. Practise until you are comfortable. Then replace the full script of the dialogue with easy-to-handle small cue cards. Keep the cue cards handy, near the telephone.

Think on your feet. Even if questions are a bit different from your prepared script, you should still be able to give short but concise answers. Accept any criticism with tact and grace. Do not lose your poise and manners on the telephone.

> ***The key to success in telephone interviews is to think on your feet.***

TRAP

Avoid salary issues. If you are asked how much money you expect, give a broad range or ask what the budgeted salary for the post is. Delay salary negotiations till you have assessed the going rate in the market for the job.

Close the conversation by showing interest and seeking a face-to-face meeting. You may say something like: "I am very interested in working for your company. I would appreciate an opportunity to meet you in person so that we can take the matter further. I am free on either ------ or -------. Which day will you prefer?"

The telephone interview is essentially a curtain-raiser. If you do well, you should expect a face-to-face meeting. How you should handle this full interview is the subject matter of the rest of this book.

4. Good Preparation is Half the Battle

What this Chapter Contains

- SWOT analysis and career planning
- Environment scanning for company information
- Using body language for interview success
- Overcoming nervousness

Don't just look at my experience. Look also at what my horoscope says about my future! JLN

Tools for Good Preparation

In the last three chapters, we have covered almost all varieties of interviews that you may face. While you do require slightly different approaches for each type, there is much in common. After all, the objective is the same in all cases. As an applicant, you have to convince the interviewer that you are the very best candidate for the job.

We look at some of the powerful preparatory tools that you can use with success, no matter what type of interview you may face, beginning with the classic three-tier variety, right down to the latest telephone interviews. These tools are:

1. SWOT analysis and career planning
2. Environment scanning for company information
3. Using body language for interview success
4. Relaxation techniques

Need for Career Planning

In today's world, it is not enough to learn just interview response skills. It is necessary to go beyond interviews and take up career planning for yourself. Time was when we grew with the organisation. We gained experience and our value to the employer increased. We contributed more and the organisation rewarded us with salary increases and promotions. Our career paths were smooth and relatively foreseeable. It was rarely necessary to do more than discharge our duties diligently. Career planning was only for the highly ambitious.

Not any more!

Rapid technology changes make our college-acquired knowledge obsolete in two to three years. Global competition forces the employer to demand better and better performance from us, year after year. Large numbers of fresh graduates enter the job market, eager to displace us. They make up for their lack of experience by their drive and ambition. Just like the industries we work for, we too face the threat of obsolescence as individuals. It is not ambition alone that drives us into conscious career planning but the sheer need for survival!

Once we recognise the need to select a career path that is in keeping with our core competence, we begin to appreciate the urgent need to add more dimensions to our interview response skills. In this chapter, we look at some of the key skills needed for career building.

The SWOT Analysis

For an assessment of our capabilities and the environment of the job market, we can use a strategic planning tool that industry has been using very successfully for a long time. This tool is called SWOT analysis. The abbreviation SWOT stands for Strengths, Weaknesses, Opportunities and Threats.

INTERNAL	Your Strengths	Your Weaknesses
EXTERNAL	Opportunities in Your Career Field	Threats in Your Career Field

Here, 'Strengths' and 'Weaknesses' apply to your 'Internal' capacity, to your personal strengths and weaknesses. For example, one of your strengths might be that you can take decisions quickly. A weakness might be that you do not always do thorough research before taking a decision.

'Opportunities' and 'Threats' apply to the external environment. For example, an opportunity might be that your organisation has recently expanded, so that there are additional openings as managers. As a result, you have a chance for a promotion. A threat might be that your organisation has begun hiring people with post-graduate degrees and you have only a bachelor's degree. Hence, you will face stiffer competition for promotions.

Perform a SWOT Analysis

Here are the steps that you follow to carry out a personal SWOT analysis:

1. **Assess your strengths**. Where do you excel? What makes you particularly useful for your targeted job? What unusual skills can you bring to the job? What part of your experience provides you depth of understanding for the work you will be required to do? What particular needs of your potential employer can you meet?

2. **Assess your weaknesses**. Where do you fall short of the needs of the advertised job? What types of tasks required for the job may be difficult for you? (For example, do you have any problem in travelling extensively?) If the job calls for teamwork, do you have any deficiency in interpersonal skills?

3. **Assess your opportunities**. What is going on in your market, your city, your state, or your country, that can benefit your selected job market? Is there a sudden rise in the demand for some skill that you have? Anything unique to you and in demand is an opportunity for you. For instance, if you know Spanish and an Indian company in your area bags an important contract in some Latin American country, it opens up an opportunity for you!

4. **Assess your threats**. How does the status of the current economy affect your targeted job market? How is your job market changing? Are any of your specialised skills becoming obsolete? Are there any changes in government legislation that may affect your job prospects? For instance, if your expertise is in the tobacco industry, there could be a slump in the business due to the government's negative stance on smoking in public places.

TIP

Select industries and organisations that can use your strengths. Plan to obtain further education and training to neutralise your weaknesses. Seek openings where your existing skills will provide you with opportunities and guard against the threat of becoming obsolete in knowledge or uncompetitive in skills in a constantly changing job market.

Scan the Environment

After obtaining an insight into your own strengths and weaknesses, you have to scan the environment of the job market around you. In this scan, you collect information about the company you are interested in as well as general information about the industry to which the company belongs. By doing a little homework beforehand, you will get to know the opportunities and threats. In addition, the knowledge you gain will help you make a good impression at the interview.

Research the Company and the Job

The more you know about the company and the job you are applying for, the better you will perform in the interview. The interviewer will be impressed by your interest and motivation and you will be able to explain convincingly just what you can do for the company.

Find out as much information as you can about the company, its products and its customers. If possible, talk to people who work at the company. There may be other sources of information on the Internet, especially if the company is listed on the stock exchange or has a Website.

Search for the following information:

- Office locations
- Products and services
- Customers
- Competitors
- Past performance record
- Recent news about expansion, mergers, performance and share price movements

> ***A company's corporate Website is an excellent source of information***

Look for an outline of the company, current projects, expansion plans etc. Websites often contain the last Annual Report. Read and learn as much as you can. This will give you an advantage when you're being interviewed because it shows that you have taken the time to find out about the company. It will also give you a bit of inside information such as who your boss would be and what kind of projects you would be working on.

Organise Your Information

It is a good idea to start collecting data as soon as you apply for an attractive job. If you get a lot of information, you will need time to sort through and retain the key facts. On the other hand, if information is hard to come by, you will have the time to dig deep for it. Either way, it will pay you to start early.

Keep a file for each application. As you do more research, the file will help you keep facts organised. When the time comes, it will make your interview preparation easier and quicker.

Each file may include cuttings from periodicals or newspapers, tips and comments from financial and business experts and annual reports. Before the interview, you can organise the information so that you have answers ready on all aspects of the company's performance and plans. Later, when you prepare your portfolio, all these will be put to good use.

TRAP

It's a mistake to assume you know enough about the organisation without doing any research. For example, you may know that Larsen & Toubro makes cement and cement plants. However, without doing research you may not know that they also undertake customised stainless steel fabrication. You may be talking with an Engineering Construction Corporation and not realise that it is a subsidiary of a much larger company (L&T) if you have not researched the company in detail.

Information Sources

You can research an organisation through a variety of sources. The primary source should be annual reports and advertisements about expansion plans, new product launches, collaborations etc.

All public limited companies are required to send annual reports to their shareholders. In addition, they have to publish six-monthly audited financial results in newspapers. Many business magazines these days regularly publish comments on company performances, particularly before a public issue of shares. The library in your city's chamber of commerce will have information on member companies.

In many cases, you can contact the organisation directly. Thereby, you will also impress the company's personnel department with your thoroughness and initiative!

Your local library should have different business periodicals and newspapers. Some of the magazines and periodicals you may want to consult are:

- *The Economic Times*
- *The Financial Times*
- *Business India*
- *The Business Week*
- *Business Today*
- *Dalal Street Journal*

There are many others. The important thing is to persist until you know the recruiting company well enough to face the interview with confidence. To test if you are sufficiently prepared, try to answer the following questions yourself:

- "What do you know about our company?"
- "Why do you want to work for us?"

Interviewers are almost certain to ask you these or similar open-ended questions. At the very least, you should be able to tell what a company's products and services are, why they interest you, and how you can contribute to these products and services.

A Two-way Street

Keep in mind that environment scanning or company research is a two-way street. You are researching information to help you get the job. In the process, you may also find things you do not like. For instance, you may come to know that the company is on the verge of a take-over. Or, a competitor with more advanced technology is about to set up a competing factory. Make sure your target is a company which you would like to work for.

> ***During company research, make sure the target is a company you would like to work for***

Body Language in Interviews

Consistency!

Having learned about yourself and the organisation interviewing you, you are well prepared with all the answers. But to sound convincing, it is as important to know what to say as it is to know how to say it. To carry conviction, your body language must back up what your lips are saying.

> ***To carry conviction, your body language must echo what your lips are saying***

TRAP You cannot avoid sending out messages through body language. It is impossible to suppress all those little movements and gestures that give you away to a trained observer. Observe another person and see how easily you can determine when he is looking bored, embarrassed or tired.

Look for small movements of head or hands, fingers or lower limbs. These are tell-tale signs that someone is exhibiting impatience or tension.

Since you cannot suppress your body language, you must train your body so that its language confirms and reinforces your verbal language. Imagine this scene. Your voice says confidently that you were the chief negotiator for your company in a wage dispute, while your body language betrays your agitation and lack of confidence! Obviously, you will not be able to carry any conviction. To succeed in interviews, therefore, you must pay special attention to your body language.

Using Body Language

To appear interested and alert, you must suppress bodily signs of tiredness and boredom. In order to appear friendly and co-operative, you must suppress spontaneous bodily reactions signifying disagreement, disbelief and aggression. While you can almost never cheat with your body, you can tone down adverse reactions and thereby improve the overall impression that you create during an interview. Body control comes with practice.

TIP

In addition to control of your own body language, it is very useful to be able to interpret the body language of the interviewer. Involuntary reactions signifying disbelief will tell you when to reinforce your claims with recorded facts (such as letters of appreciation). Similarly, signs of boredom will tell you when to cut short a long narration or to change the topic. If you observe signs of disagreement, or even aggression, when you are expressing an opinion, be warned. It will be best not to pursue the topic!

Observe and Interpret Body Language

While everyone notices and interprets body language naturally, some are more sensitive than others. Even if you are not naturally very sensitive, you can develop an ability to control your own body language and understand that of others. You can do so by study and through observation, just as you would for spoken languages.

You can make the most of your opportunities for observation and practice in everyday situations. If you know the person you are observing, you can verify the accuracy of your interpretation by asking verbal questions about his or her reaction. Your understanding of body language will not only make you a better candidate at an interview, but will also greatly improve your interpersonal communication skills.

Overcoming Nervousness

It's normal to be nervous before job interviews, but some job seekers go to extremes. They are so fearful and apprehensive that they become tongue-tied. They end up by either talking too much or forget all the facts and figures that they had carefully studied. Needless to say, the interview does not go according to plan!

Most experts agree that a manageable level of stress can actually improve interview performance. "It quickens our mind, sharpens our conversation and pumps more adrenaline into our system," says an expert on motivation and self-confidence. He goes on to add, "At zero level of tension, there are no concerns and no arousal. Therefore, you are not keyed up to perform well." But if your blood pressure rises too much and your palms become too clammy, you need to control your reactions.

> ***A manageable level of tension before an interview will actually improve your performance***

The key to calmness is learning not to exaggerate an interview's importance. Lowering the stakes can reduce your stress level considerably.

TRAP

In contrast, if you believe that you must succeed at all costs, your tension level will soar. You will be a self-conscious spectator of your own behaviour, watching and judging every word during the interview. Not only does this make you less convincing and more anxious, it also distracts you from all the facts and figures that you have so carefully learned.

Do not behave like a perfectionist who cannot bear to fail. If you do, you will become very self-conscious and will not be able to project the easy, confident and eager demeanour so important for interview success. Excessive self-consciousness can not only prevent individuals from responding to questions with confidence, it can actually cause them to perform well below their actual capabilities.

Reducing Interview Tension

If you are too anxious, even your advance preparation can be affected. You will tend to be over-prepared. As a result, your spontaneity will be lost and you will lose your flexibility. Both of these are necessary to think on your feet and answer unexpected questions confidently and convincingly.

Here are some comforting thoughts and advice on interviews:

- Interviews centre on the subject you know best, which is yourself. If you have done your homework, you have an advantage; you know more about the interviewer and his company than he or she knows about you. Therefore, you should have confidence in your ability to handle the situation.
- Remind yourself that whatever happens, you will live to fight another day. The less you worry about making mistakes, the less anxious you will be. Anticipating and worrying about an unpleasant experience is always worse than the experience itself.
- Try to generate several interview calls so you will not rest all your hopes on one of them. "With backups in mind, you will feel more relaxed going in, and you'll actually stand a better chance of landing the job," says a career counselling expert. "Potential employers are quick to spot desperation and are turned off by it."
- Never confront interviewers, regardless of how tense you may feel. Instead of making them the butt of your misdirected anxiety, tell yourself that they are only human and treat them as your friends.

Relaxation Techniques

To reduce stress, some candidates practise relaxation exercises before interviews. Here is a very successful technique. Visualise a serene and beautiful scene, such as a moonlit beach. Become aware of your breathing rhythm. As you inhale, think: "I am." When you exhale, think:

"Calm." Breathe at least 10 times, then recall a past successful interview experience.

Here is a more advanced breathing technique, adapted from yogic breathing exercises. Relax and exhale completely. Next, close your mouth and place the thumb of your right hand on your right nostril so that it is completely closed. Then slowly and deeply inhale and exhale through your left nostril at least 25 to 30 times. It is claimed that this allows you to tap into the right hemisphere of your brain, particularly the limbic part that governs emotions. You will experience an immediate reduction in anxiety and feel more relaxed and controlled during the interview.

A yogic technique for relaxation

Power of Visualisation

Another way to reduce stress is to visualise how you want to appear to the interviewer. Separate yourself from your performance. Develop an image of an ideal executive or perfect candidate for the job. Model your behaviour after this image. Just as an actor or actress creates the character from the script, you must try to create a character for the position you seek. The trick is to create a memory based on past success.

Visualise an ideal character. One you would like to be at the interview

Here is how you start a visualisation session:

- Find a tranquil, quiet place where you will be totally undisturbed. Purge your mind of ordinary concerns, worries and preoccupations. Eliminate thoughts that are not directly pertinent to your visualisation and find a quiet mental space. Lie down with legs uncrossed and arms by your sides. Close your eyes and inhale slowly, expanding your chest and lower abdomen. Pause for a moment. Then exhale slowly and relax your chest and abdomen. Inhale and exhale until you feel deeply relaxed. As you become more tranquil, breathe more slowly and evenly.

- Next, believe that the interview is already over, and you have been selected. Focus your will and energy on this visualisation. See it clearly enough to believe that it is real. Picture yourself after completing the interview. What would you be doing? Feeling? Saying? Use all of your senses to experience the consequences of successfully completing the interview.
- Finally, believe that you deserve to have a successful interview. Talk positively to yourself about your value to an employer and why you should be selected.

Repeat the sessions at least thrice before the actual interview, visualising as long as you like. With repeated visualisations you can enrich the scenes with more detail and make the outcome very believable.

Interviews are experiences that improve with practice. As your fear subsides, you will perform better. You will gain confidence in your interview skills. Eventually, you will perform as well as the ideal person you had visualised in your mind at the start of the exercise.

5. Your Make-over and Portfolio

WHAT THIS CHAPTER CONTAINS

- Dressing appropriately for the interview
- Attire for men
- Attire for women
- The value of a portfolio
- Professional and job portfolios

Ok! Ok! Another thousand per month!

From Contents to Packaging

We move from the contents to its packaging in this chapter. In the last chapter, we focussed on information that you collect about yourself and the company. This provides the information content for your interview. However, what you say will be influenced a great deal by how you appear to the interviewers. Therefore, your appearance is important. You need to package yourself attractively to succeed in interviews. By packaging, we mean the way you look, the way you dress and groom yourself, even what you carry with you, so that your image creates the best possible impression.

In this chapter we will look at how you can "make yourself over" by dressing, grooming and organising the things you carry to the interview in a way that truly showcases you. Think of this chapter as a 'finishing school' for you! In the first part we will cover dressing and grooming. In the second part, we will tell you what to carry with you and how to package this in your professional and job portfolios.

When you read this chapter, also keep in mind what we discussed in Chapter 4, *Good Preparation is Half the Battle*, regarding your body language.

Dressing for Interview Success

The clothes you wear to the interview will create a strong first impression. If you wear the right clothes, you will be perceived in a more positive light by your interviewer. But if you wear clothes that are inappropriate for the type of job you have applied for, you will almost certainly lose your chance.

For both men and women, the safest option is to select conservative clothes that project a reliable, dependable and conservative image. Therefore, avoid anything that may appear too flashy or too trendy.

In almost all interview situations, very casual clothes such as sandals and T-shirts are completely inappropriate, even though the employees of the interviewing company may adopt a casual style.

TIP

Pointed-toe shoes generally known as 'Oxfords' and business suits are still the most appropriate wear for interviews. In our country, due to the weather, there is a great temptation to dispense with the necktie. However, for almost all job interviews for men, neckties are considered not only appropriate, but necessary. This is especially true if the job you are seeking involves contact with customers or clients.

Unfortunately, most college graduates do not possess an appropriate wardrobe. There are economic reasons for trying to get by with what you already have. Proper dress, however, is as important as your educational degree to succeed in interviews. You need not buy an entirely new wardrobe. Just one well-chosen business suit for men or a sari ensemble for women will serve you all the way through the interviews to the first day on the job.

In an interview, you should be doing the talking, not your clothes!

If you desire some variety within a limited budget, you might consider varying your shirt/blouse/tie or accessories as a simple way to change your look without blowing a hole in your pocket. Remember, however, that stylish is not conservative. You should be doing the talking in an interview, not your clothes.

Pay particular attention to your shoes. Well-maintained and neatly polished shoes display attention to detail and diligence, factors that employers will value.

Some professional recruiters believe that they can judge a person by their shoes. You will find that ex-military officers, many of whom have found their way into management positions in civilian life, are especially aware of a person's shoes. It is not enough to be clean, pressed, and ironed. Make sure your shoes are conservative, clean, and polished as well.

Interview Attire for Men

Interviewers will judge you within the first five minutes of an interview. If you appear clean, neat and polished, you will make a good impression. Here are some specific suggestions on attire:

Suits: Choose colours from navy blue up to dark (teal) blue and charcoal. At the other end of the scale, you may select light grey. Avoid very sharp contrasts such as black suits with white shirts and black ties. It is too formal and more appropriate for a funeral. Brown and beige can also be selected, but blue/greys are preferred. Solid colours are best, but muted or narrow pinstripes are also acceptable. Choose all-wool or wool blended with man-made fibres that will drape well on you.

Shirts: Short sleeve shirts are inappropriate for interviews. Wear a white or light-coloured shirt. A current fashion is to wear a dark shirt like dark (teal) blue, maroon or navy blue, contrasted with a coordinated dark tie. In general, for executive jobs, err on the side of being conservative. However, if you are being interviewed for a selling or counselling position, then you may look for less muted colour combinations. In any case, keep away from patterned shirts and monograms.

Ties: Select pure silk ties. They do not crease as easily and, therefore, look neat and professional. Ties should complement your outfit and not clash with it. Therefore, choose a tie that blends in colour and pattern with the rest of your suit. Select one with a striped, paisley or a small pattern such as dots. Avoid large, elaborate patterns or ties with more than two or three colours.

Shoes: Shoes should be black leather lace-ups, not sandals or moccasins. A safe choice is pointed-toe Oxfords. Make sure your shoes are polished and in good condition. You could get away with brown leather, but black is considered more professional.

Socks: Your socks should complement your suit. Generally, look for colours such as dark blue, black, grey, brown or beige. Whatever the colours, your socks should be long enough so that if you cross your legs, no bare skin shows. Make sure that the elastic on the top of your socks will keep them pulled up taut. Wrinkled, saggy socks will undo all the good work done by the rest of your wardrobe!

Accessories: A simple, plain analogue watch is acceptable. Remove all other jewellery except for your very personal items such as your wedding ring. Cuff links are acceptable so long as they are simple. Avoid anything with a very large or striking motif. If you have a neck chain or earring, be sure to leave them home on the day of the interview! If you have a briefcase it should be in black, brown or beige leather, as plain as possible. Later in this chapter, we will describe a portfolio that you may want to carry instead of a bulky briefcase. Use a belt rather than suspenders. Your belt should complement your shoes and suit. Black or brown is preferable.

Grooming: Have a haircut, preferably a couple of days before the interview. Short hair is the best. A clean-shaven look is the safest unless you are being auditioned as a model! Avoid beards altogether. Moustaches should also be avoided. If not, make sure they are neatly trimmed. Fingernails should be clean and trimmed. Make sure there are no chipped nails.

Perfumes: It is best to use only after-shave lotions and/or deodorants for men. Select subtle ones, not ones that can be smelt ten feet away. While you do want to suppress body odour, do not smell like a perfume factory!

TIP

Always remember to wear a cotton vest under your shirt even in hot weather, since it makes the shirt look whiter. Take your shirt to a commercial laundry or dry cleaner and ask for starch to be used. Invariably, professionally laundered shirts look much better than what you can manage at home. Put on a shirt which is fresh from the cleaners just before the interview. Check your suit to see if it needs pressing and keep your shoes freshly polished.

Interview Attire for Women

Remember that one's dress and grooming send out powerful messages to a prospective employer. Clinging clothes, purple or glittery fingernails, excessive perfumes or anything that calls loud attention to you is inappropriate for an interview. Whether long or short, your hair must be neatly groomed and firmly in place. You must project a picture of control, efficiency and muted elegance. Flamboyance may be appropriate in a fashion show, but is out of place in an interview room.

Yet, you cannot afford to look dowdy. Striking a balance between being uninteresting and too interesting is an art. Before an important interview, you may do well to take professional advice on your appearance and grooming. Given below are some basic tips and pointers to help you with your personal make-over style.

> ***Strike a balance between being dowdy and too flamboyant***

The traditional formal attire for women in India is a sari ensemble. However, many young professionals prefer to wear a business suit (jacket and skirt) to create an efficient image. The final choice is yours.

TRAP

If you have never worn a business suit before, it is not a good idea to wear one especially for your interview. You will be far too self-conscious in this unfamiliar attire. You must be at ease and confident, so that you are at your best in the interview. Stick to what you are familiar with and comfortable in.

The first item in the list of hints and tips that follow is for a sari ensemble. The second is for a business suit. Skirts, stockings and shoes go with a business suit. The other hints and tips will apply both to suits and saris.

Sari Ensemble: Silks are preferable to cotton, unless weather does not permit you to wear anything heavier than cotton. Select dark shades with contrasting borders and *pallu*. However, you must avoid striking colour contrasts. What may be attractive as an evening party wear will be too loud for an interview. It is preferable to wear a white silk blouse with half or three-quarter sleeves and a U-neck of conservative cut. Positively avoid sleeveless blouses or ones with a plunging neckline. If you select a sari ensemble, ignore the tips regarding shoes since you will wear sandals. Your sandals should not be high heeled or with a wide, open front that displays all your toes. For the rest of your attire, follow the guidelines listed after Suits below.

Suits: With a huge range of options available to women, it is much easier for them to make a fashion mistake at an interview. Look for a business style suit with a jacket, knee-length skirt in grey, charcoal, black, navy blue or maroon. Try to avoid patterned material for the clothes you wear. A cotton-synthetic blend is probably the best kind of fabric, but you may also look for wool blends or micro fibres. Look for drape, fall and crease resistance.

A classic suit in navy blue, grey or black is always appropriate. Instead of dark colours, you can select khaki in summer. Although a suit is preferable, a navy-blue blazer and classic grey skirt made of wool in winter or linen in summer can be an alternative. It is generally advisable to wear skirts instead of pants. Many experts believe that pants are seen to be too aggressive and "bossy" by some male interviewers.

Some male interviewers view pants as too aggressive and "bossy"

Skirts: A word about skirt lengths is in order. Shorter skirts are acceptable provided that the skirt meets the top of the knee. We do not, however, advise anyone to go for an interview in a short skirt unless you are looking for a position in the fashion industry. In traditionally male-dominated fields, such as banking and the law, miniskirts and skirts with high slits are not advisable.

Blouses: Long sleeves are the best option and again, white, cream or soft pastel colours are your best choice. Avoid linen as it creases; choose something that is blended with a synthetic fabric that will not crease. As for the blouse, we suggest a white or ivory cotton shade with high neck, which is appropriate for suits. As an alternative, you could select silk or polyester that looks like silk. For blouses that go with a sari ensemble, see the paragraph under Sari Ensemble earlier in this chapter.

Scarves: A pure silk scarf in a colour or pattern that blends with your blouse can give you a conservative look. But be careful to avoid any outlandish or loud fabrics. In warm weather, you may wish to add the scarf just before entering the interview room.

Stockings: These are essential with skirts. Choose skin-coloured tones and avoid anything that shines or calls attention to your legs. Be prepared for last-minute ladders and runs. Carry another pair in your handbag for a last-minute replacement if required.

Accessories: Keep your jewellery down to a minimum. Plain earrings and necklace and your wedding or engagement rings are acceptable. Do not have every finger covered with a ring. Generally, one ring on both hands should be the limit. The important thing is to wear just a few pieces of jewellery. You want to look elegant yet efficient, not opulent!

Leather Accessories: Select a brown, black or maroon leather briefcase. If you want to wear a belt, make sure it blends in with your suit. You could try black or brown. Your belt should complement or match your shoes. What you should avoid, however, is carrying a shopping bag to an interview. As an alternative to a briefcase, you may select a portfolio bag. We will discuss portfolios in the next section.

Shoes: These should be leather, preferably in black or brown. Stay away from ultra-trendy shoes and bright colours. A simple court shoe or pump is probably the best choice. In case of a sari ensemble, select sandals instead of pumps.

Makeup: Your aim is to create a subtle and natural aura about yourself. Make sure you do not have a foundation line around your jaw. Select natural shades for your eye shadow and lipstick. Make sure that none of the nail polish is chipped and the colour is clear pink or red. Take a lipstick with you if you need to freshen up before you are called in for the interview. Perfume or cologne should be muted and understated. Select a suitable light fragrance and use it sparingly.

Here are a few additional tips to help you look calm, confident and elegant!

- Make sure your pockets are empty. There should be no bulges or tinkling coins, no gum, candy or cigarettes in your pockets.

- With the exception of earrings, avoid anything that may highlight visible body piercing such as nose-rings, eyebrow rings etc. Avoid dangling earrings that move with every movement of your head. It can be distracting.
- If you need to wear athletic shoes en route to the interview, carry a briefcase large enough to conceal them. Change into your pumps or sandals before you enter the office of the interviewer.

Your Portfolio

In this competitive world where applicants vastly outnumber the available jobs, it is easy to appreciate the vital importance of standing out from the rest of the field. The need is easily understood, but apart from counting on good qualifications and past track record, it is not easy to think of other ways to appear outstanding. If your qualifications and experience are not so exceptional, should you leave things to fate or try something really innovative?

A well-compiled portfolio will help you stand out from the crowd

Here is an idea. Try to compile and use a job portfolio in your next interview to highlight your talents and achievements. Your portfolio will give you the potential and power to distinguish yourself from the competition.

Think of your portfolio as a scrapbook, binder, or album. It is a collection of the tangible proof of your past and recent work, achievements in volunteer or community work, educational and personal accomplishments and talents. Think of it also as a way to display all the strengths you have listed in your résumé and will describe in your interviews.

Portfolios are already in common use by artists, photographers, architects, designers and writers in search of work. They have used portfolios to showcase their abilities and their style very successfully for quite a while. Now, other professionals in business and industry are rediscovering portfolios. A good example of this is the new breed of information technology professionals who take contract jobs and move on after their assignment is over.

What is a Portfolio?

Your professional portfolio is a collection of items or artefacts. It is a place where you store things related to your training, work experience, contributions, and special accomplishments. It is the place where you record all your work-related talents and accomplishments so that you can display these assets to the interviewer.

Since each one of us has a unique professional career, it follows that no two portfolios will be quite the same. However, all portfolios will usually have a number of sections. These include:

- A copy of your résumé
- Educational data including copies of degrees, diplomas and certificates; evidence of professional development such as conferences and training courses attended
- Job history with details of employers, positions held and major successes
- Evidence of your achievements, volunteer experience, community work
- Evidence of reports, publications, honours and awards
- Your personal mission statement, career and personal goals

The following list is by no means exhaustive. However, if you are preparing your professional portfolio for the first time, you should find almost all that you are likely to need in this list:

Personal

- Birth certificate
- Driver's licence
- Any other licences or identifying documents such as voter's card or PAN card

- Health records
- Passport/Citizenship papers

Education and Extra-curricular

- Schools attended
- Diplomas, certificates, licences
- Assessments, test results, appraisals, mark sheets
- Internships, apprenticeships, special projects
- Workshops, seminars, conferences attended
- Independent learning, things you have learned on your own, or taught yourself
- Special training that you may have received
- Activities, hobbies or interests, with photographs
- Participation in team sports
- Para-military or military training including citations and complete description of duties and activities
- Volunteer activities
- Organisations joined
- Public speaking or public performance details
- Awards

Work Related

- Jobs/contracts held. Include job title, description of all duties, supervisor's name, your phone and address
- Performance reports, appraisals
- Accomplishments and awards
- Publications, reports, published articles
- Organisation charts

- Documentation of accomplishments – increases in sales, decrease in claims
- Major projects completed/participated in

While you accumulate your professional portfolio, your focus is yourself, things you know, things you can do, things that describe you, who and what you are.

TIP

From the professional portfolio, you assemble a job portfolio for a specific interview, selecting only relevant things, using your résumé and your knowledge of the recruiting company as a guide. A specific job portfolio will therefore be only a smaller sub-set of your professional portfolio.

Benefits of a Portfolio

Some candidates will get jobs without preparing a portfolio and you may hear from others that no one really wanted to see their portfolio during the interview. You will also hear from others that their portfolio was a major factor in getting a job.

You must remember that many interviewers become tired of merely hearing about a candidate's skills or reading about them in a résumé. A portfolio contains evidence that your skills and abilities actually exist. While some interviewers will be impressed by the fact that you have taken the time and effort to compile a portfolio, others will want to take a look at how well you document your abilities. Still others will want to discuss with you what you have included and why.

A portfolio contains evidence to back up your claims

It is important to remember that even if you do not get the opportunity to show your portfolio to an interviewer, the process of organising and reviewing your abilities and experiences will help you prepare for the interviews, and to write

The process of preparing your portfolio is an excellent way to prepare for interviews

your résumé. The reflective thinking and rehearsing you do to prepare a quality portfolio may be the most effective step in your career building.

The Professional Portfolio

For your professional portfolio, you have to cast your net far and wide. Here is a step-by-step procedure that you may follow:

1. Gather together all those crucial letters and documents you have been saving somewhere.

2. Purchase a good-sized binder for the professional portfolio. It may have three rings or separate zippered compartments; it may be bound in leather or cloth. You can be as creative as you want.

3. Also buy several smaller folders which are inexpensive but businesslike. They are for individual job portfolios.

4. Gather together sheet protectors sealed on the bottom so items do not fall out. Find some blank labels for item description and section dividers with labels and good-quality plain paper for duplicating documents. You can add multimedia items such as CD-ROMs or floppy disks, if necessary.

5. Place each item in a plastic sheet protector. For two-sided documents, display the pages back-to-back in one protector. Identify key sections with labels and avoid punching holes in the documents themselves. Use the holes in the plastic sheet protector for filing.

6. Arrange each section chronologically. For instance, the section dealing with education will normally come before the section on job experience. Use the sequence in your résumé as a guide.

The Job Portfolio

You should not take your entire professional portfolio to an interview. Instead, you should extract exactly what is necessary to include in a job portfolio specifically assembled for each individual interview.

To organise a job portfolio, identify the skill requirements of the job. Now identify your skills, accomplishments and qualifications that meet the job's needs. Finally, select those documents from the professional portfolio that support your claims for being a suitable candidate for the job. If you have organised your professional portfolio with care, the matching should not be difficult.

It is easy to extract individual job portfolios if your professional portfolio has been assembled with care

Finally, photocopy the selected documents and arrange them in appropriate sections in the job portfolio. Make sure that the sequence matches the sequence of information in your résumé so that any reader can relate the two easily. Now you have an attractive document that confirms the claims you have made in your résumé and will provide support for what you will highlight during the interview. Take this shorter, focussed job portfolio to interviews and produce it to illustrate your relevant skills.

A well-matched résumé and portfolio make a winning combination!

TIP

If you carry only photocopies of the originals, you can leave the job portfolio behind with the interviewer to continue to work on your behalf even after the interview is over.

Final Thoughts

One of the major problems that fresh graduates face in preparing an impressive résumé is the apparent lack of success stories. If you put together a professional portfolio with care, you will be surprised at the amount of evidence you can accumulate testifying to your achievements. All this will help you prepare an impressive résumé, boost your self-confidence and ultimately get you the career move that you desire.

Similarly, some of us who have gaps in our employment history may find evidence of useful things we did between jobs to further our education or gain useful experience. Portfolio preparation will help you

> ***Portfolio preparation helps you fill embarrassing gaps in your education or employment history***

dig out vital evidence in support of these achievements and, suddenly, the gaps will no longer be embarrassments for you.

In this section you have learned something quite unusual – how to collect and organise all those items and achievements that reflect so much about you. They have always had a place in your heart and mind. Now get them out in the open and put them to work for you, in your portfolio!

6. The Big Moment is Here!

What this Chapter Contains

- Preparations on the day before the interview
- Practising with mock interviews
- Calming your nerves
- Handling yourself during the interview
- Questions to expect and questions to ask
- Handling stress situations

Yes! I can see how your BIG resume will fit in with our company's BIG expansion plans!

JLN

The Day Before

This is the day before your interview. You are now ready for the battle to begin. Tomorrow, all your knowledge and preparation will be put to the test! You should have gone through Chapter 4, devoted entirely to preparation for the interview. Here are some additional tips appropriate for the day before the interview.

Common Questions

Prepare answers to the common questions asked at interviews. If you have been to an interview before, you will know the type of queries we are talking about. Questions often asked include:

- Why do you want to work for our company?
- What are your strengths and weaknesses?
- How would you describe yourself?
- Are you a team player or an individualist?
- How can you benefit our company?
- Tell me about yourself?
- What do you like to do outside work hours?

For more practice questions and questions with model answers, see Chapter 9, *Frequently Asked Questions*, later in this book.

Negative Aspects

Evaluate negative aspects of your résumé such as:

- Limited education, experience or skills
- Long-term absence from workforce
- Many job changes within a short time

In each case, develop positive and plausible responses to questions about them. In Chapter 10, *Pitfalls to Avoid*, you will see how you can compensate for weaknesses in your resume. See Chapter 9, *Frequently*

Asked Questions, as well for more typical questions and model answers. Go through these to get ideas and then prepare answers appropriate for your case.

Mock Interview

Conduct a mock interview with a friend. Prepare a list of job requirements for your friend to see. Prepare another list of the negative aspects of your résumé as we have just discussed. Try to emphasise your accomplishments and skills that meet the needs of the job. Answer questions on your negative aspects as well. Ask your friend for constructive suggestions at the end of the mock interview. The suggestions should highlight:

- How well you projected yourself as the best candidate for the job
- How well you answered difficult questions
- What was the overall impression you created
- Are there any mannerisms, hesitations, gestures or body language that will appear negative to an interviewer?

Practise any last-minute correction that this mock interview throws up. By doing so, you will build up your confidence since you know that you have corrected the shortcomings in your preparation.

All that remains now is to familiarise yourself with the location of the interview and plan to reach 10 to 15 minutes early. Bring several copies of your résumé and one copy of your job portfolio to the interview. See Chapter 5, *Your Make-over and Portfolio*, for more information on how to prepare your professional and job portfolios.

Calm Your Nerves

Refer to the last section in Chapter 4, *Good Preparation is Half the Battle*, for hints and tips on calming your nerves and reducing your tension. If you have been following the recommendations in this book so far, you should have:

- Carried out a SWOT analysis to get an objective picture of your strengths and weaknesses
- Collected relevant information about the job and the company
- Made sure of your dress and grooming
- Prepared a specific portfolio for this interview
- Practised with mock interviews to perfect your technique
- Calmed yourself and built up your self-confidence

If you have done so, you can be sure you will be one of the best candidates, if not the best, to turn up for the interview! You are prepared, pumped up and ready to face any interview board ever constituted! You really do not have anything to worry about. Go and ace that interview!

Opening Moves

Tips for the Day of the Interview

Plan to arrive 15 minutes early. Be sure to allot enough time for bad traffic conditions.

Dress to impress. Make sure that your attire is well pressed and wrinkle free. Remember that you can never look too professional for an interview. All the tips you need about dressing and grooming are in Chapter 5, *Your Make-over & Portfolio.*

Try to relax and approach the interview as if you already have the job. Remember what we discussed in Chapter 4, *Good Preparation is Half the Battle*, regarding the power of visualisation. Visualise yourself in a winning position!

Beginning the Interview

Offer a firm and brief handshake. Be natural and spontaneous but not hearty or familiar. Handshaking appropriately is one act that you should practise with friends before an interview. We do not always shake hands as a greeting in India. Therefore, we may be too timid or too hearty out of unfamiliarity and nervousness. Practise a firm, friendly yet businesslike handshake.

A poor handshake can get your interview off to a bad start!

TRAP

Maintain good eye contact. If your eyes drop all the time, you will appear too timid. If your eyes slide away before you answer, you will look shifty and your answers may not carry any conviction. On the other hand, trying to stare the interviewer down is a very bad strategy. It will provoke antagonism in the interviewer. Like handshaking, proper eye contact requires practise.

Show interest in the company and the position being offered to you. If you realise early in the interview that the job does not meet your expectations, try to wind up the discussion politely. Indicate that you need time to think over the matter. Make sure that you thank the interviewer for his or her time. There is always the possibility that you may seek another interview with this organisation at some future date. Leave on a pleasant note.

Even if the job does not meet your expectations, conclude the interview gracefully

Do pay full attention to the interviewer and listen closely to what is being said. This advice is particularly important if you are feeling nervous or excited. In such a situation, you may find that you are jumping the gun, that is, answering even before the question has been completed. Unlike the buzzer round in a quiz contest, there are no bonus points for trying to answer too quickly!

There are no bonus points for answering too quickly!

Do show enthusiasm and confidence in yourself. You have prepared thoroughly, dressed well, have a portfolio that few may have thought of and you are really keen to get this job. These feelings of eagerness and self-confidence will come through in the way you speak and in your body language creating a confident and competent image.

Do be honest about questions asked. Even if the question points to an area of weakness, you must learn to reply adroitly, without using untruths.

Consider an example. Let us assume that you are asked, "What are your weaknesses?" You can answer the question rather flippantly by saying, "Oh! I do not know. I have never thought about it." Such an answer shows that you do not have an in-depth understanding of your skills or personal strengths. Here is a much better, well thought out response. Say, "Well, some people have said that I can be a bit quiet, but at the same time, I am a good listener. Sometimes this may be mistaken as being 'quiet'. However, I do know that I have to work on being a little more outgoing."

Work on a few questions like this to have good answers ready whenever you may need them. See Chapter 9, *Frequently Asked Questions*, for more examples.

Do remember to switch off cell phones, pagers or alarms on your wristwatch if you happen to have any of these. At the interview, your entire focus of attention is the interview itself and all your actions must confirm this.

During the Interview

In General

Show self-confidence. Make eye contact with the interviewer and answer his questions in a clear voice. Try to establish a rapport with the interviewer. You have to focus your attention on the interviewer's manner and speed. Is he or she asking crisp, rapid-fire questions? If so, keep your answers short and to the point. On the other hand, if the interviewer is relaxed and takes time to ask the next question, you should speak in a similar manner and tone. While you could elaborate on your answers as required, do not stray from the point.

Remember to listen. Else, you will miss important cues from the interviewer

Communication is a two-way street. If you are talking too much, you will probably miss cues concerning what the interviewer feels are important to him or her. Reflect before answering a difficult question.

TOP

If you are unsure how to answer a question, you might reply with another question. For example, if the interviewer asks you what salary you expect, try answering by saying, "I have to give it some thought. What are you planning to pay your best candidate?"

See Chapter 8, *Salary Negotiations*, for more salary-related questions and answers.

Ask Pertinent Questions

When it is your turn, ask the questions you have prepared in advance. These should cover any information about the company and job that you could not find in your own research.

TRAP

Do not ask questions that raise question marks about your enthusiasm. For example, if you ask whether all jobs are transferable without the topic coming up at all, the interviewer may assume that you do not want to be transferred under any circumstances. This is a rather rigid attitude and will work against you. Similarly, raising too many questions about holidays and perquisites in the very first interview may cause the interviewer to think that you are more interested in benefits than the challenges the job has to offer.

At this stage of the interview, it is your abilities and your can-do attitude that need to be highlighted. You must show that you want the job. Display your initiative by talking about what you could do to benefit the organisation. Give specific details of how you have helped past employers. If you have prepared your job portfolio with care, you would have found examples of past successes that should benefit the organisation interviewing you.

Do ask specific details of the job, such as functions, responsibilities, who you would work with, and who you will report to. When these details are being discussed, you will see opportunities of mentioning some specific skill or ability of yours that should benefit the organisation. Do not miss these chances to showcase your fitness for the job. Your intention is to show how you can start producing results for the organisation right away.

> ***Do not miss any opportunity to highlight your fitness for the job***

Handling Stress Situations

It is natural to feel anxious and stressed at an interview. Part of the anxiety is due to your burning desire to succeed. Part of the disquiet may also be due to deliberate action on the part of the interviewer to test how you stand up under stress. In the second half of Chapter 4, *Good Preparation is Half the Battle*, earlier in this book, we have discussed a few effective ways to relax before the interview. In addition to these techniques, here are some tips to combat interview-related stress.

Recognise the situation as a test of your self-control and not as a personal attack on you. If you are facing a stressful interview, remember that most probably all the other candidates with potential will also be subjected to a similar test. If you respond better than the others, you gain a valuable edge over them. Therefore, a stress test is also an opportunity for you to stand out from the competition if you can handle the situation with finesse.

> ***Stress interviews are a test of your self-control and not a personal attack on you***

It is important that you do not allow your body language to betray that you are agitated or threatened. Learn how to control your body so that it does not betray you at a crucial point in your interview. Recognise these signs of nervousness or tension and control them consciously:

- Frequently touching your mouth or gnawing your lip

- Faking a cough so you have time to think about the answer to a question
- Wearing a tight or forced smile and avoiding eye contact
- Swinging your foot or leg
- Folding or crossing your arms
- Slouching and sinking back in your seat
- Picking at invisible bits of lint from your clothes

For a more detailed understanding of body language, see the second half of Chapter 4, *Good Preparation is Half the Battle*, earlier in this book.

Be Yourself

Convey your strengths and abilities without appearing boastful or conceited. Do not exaggerate, but do emphasise areas where your expertise matches the needs of the job.

> ***If you succeed in hoodwinking the interviewer, you may get a job for which you are neither qualified nor capable!***

Answer the questions honestly, rather than telling the interviewer what you think he or she wants to hear. Exaggeration and/or boasting is a very bad strategy. If you do succeed in hoodwinking the interviewer, you may end up by getting a job for which you are neither qualified nor capable!

Instead, try to show genuine enthusiasm and display an engaging personality. Remember to smile.

Volunteer information only if it is positive and pertinent. Avoid using negative terms. Make use of words like “challenge” or “opportunity” instead of calling something a “problem”. Never forget that your objective is to get a job offer suited to your skills and qualifications.

Closing the Interview

The darkest night and the longest interview will eventually end! No matter how stressful the experience, you will display your quality and staying power if you handle the entire interview with dignity and end the encounter with grace.

TIP

End the interview with a handshake and thank the interviewer for his or her time. Reiterate your interest in the position and your qualifications for the job. Ask if you can telephone in a few days to check on your status. If they offer to contact you, politely ask when you should expect the call.

After the interview, send a brief thank-you note. Try to time it so it reaches before the hiring decision will be made. It will serve as a reminder to the interviewer concerning your suitability for the position, so feel free to mention any topics discussed during your interview. If the initial contact was made through the Internet, do e-mail a thank-you note immediately after the interview. Follow up with a phone call if you are not contacted within a week of the date when the interviewer said that you would be contacted.

For more details on post-interview follow-up, see Chapter 7, *Follow-up and Offer Evaluation.*

7. Follow-up and Offer Evaluation

WHAT THIS CHAPTER CONTAINS

- The thank-you letter
- Seeking help from your referees
- How to generate job offers
- Offer evaluation techniques
- Declining unsuitable offers gracefully

We urgently need salesmen to sell refrigerators to ESKIMOS!

Effective Follow-up

The interview is finally over! You heave a sigh of relief. There is a feeling of accomplishment as you have completed a difficult task well. So, all you have to do you now is relax and await a job offer. Right? Wrong! Possibly you are but one of at least two or three short-listed candidates and the final selection is yet to be made. So the battle for the job continues. You have prepared an excellent portfolio and you performed really well in the interview; now you have to ensure that all the good work done so far is not undone due to lack of follow-up.

> ***In spite of a very good interview, lack of effective follow-up may yet cost you the job***

Here are some guidelines for effective follow-up. We begin with your thank-you letter and the help you can seek from your references. We move on to a discussion on how to handle multiple offers and how to evaluate them so that you can pick what is best for you. Techniques of salary negotiations, however, deserve an entire chapter to themselves. They are covered in Chapter 8, *Salary Negotiations*.

The Thank-you Letter

As soon as you come out of the Interview room, before you leave the premises, pull out a thank-you note that you should bring specifically for this purpose. Fill in the details and hand it to the receptionist on your way out with a request that it should be given to the interviewer(s).

If it is not possible to prepare and deliver a note in person for some reason, then send a note by mail the very next day, thanking the interviewers for their time and for giving you the opportunity to meet them. Do this even if you are not interested in the job. You never know where you might run into them again. Get the names of the interviewers from the receptionist and make sure that you spell them right!

During the interview ask the interviewer how long it would be before the outcome is known. If you do not hear from them after this waiting period, call them to confirm your continued interest in the job.

Ideally, your thank-you letter should be in the hands of the interviewers by the end of the day of the interview or early the following morning. It is important to remind them about yourself while the impression you have made is still fresh in their minds.

TIP

Not everyone follows up like this. In most cases, no one calls up after an interview and few take the time to write a thank-you letter. Therefore, by the simple gesture of a phone call and thank-you letter, you can stand out from the competition.

Seek Help from Your Referees

To make a lasting impression on a potential employer, ask the individuals or referees who supplied you with letters of recommendation to either call or write to the employer after your interview, giving their personal recommendations. Unsolicited recommendations usually make a major impact on the employer.

TRAP

This technique works only if you have a strong sponsor or two among your referees. Even if you know that a referee is likely to oblige, use caution. Avoid asking recommendations for each and every job application. Instead, save this request for a really important job, where you feel that the interview has gone very well, and a word will positively tilt the balance in your favour.

If you decide to use this technique, persuade the referee to write an original letter on his or her stationary or letterhead. Do not use a standard, pre-written letter that you send to your referee, asking him to merely sign and post it to your employer. If your referee does this, there is truly no higher compliment that he or she can pay you. So do remember to thank him or her, in words now, and with a card and a small gift when you do get the job.

Generating Job Offers

Once the thank-you letter has been sent, your aim is to ensure you get an offer. For effective follow-up, stay in touch with your primary contact in the employer's office. Your primary contact will usually be someone in their personnel department with whom you have already spoken or corresponded. By staying in touch with this person, you will remain aware of the progress of your case. You will also keep the organisation aware of your continuing interest. Get in touch at least once a week. There is no reason for your enquiries to be misunderstood. If you were interested enough to prepare and perform well at the interview, it follows that you will continue to be interested in the job.

For effective follow-up, it is important to remain in close touch with the interviewing company

Be straightforward and direct in your queries and the contact should keep you posted about your progress. If you are no longer under consideration, you will be informed. If there are further interviews pending or your background is being reviewed by others, you will be informed. If the company is getting ready to put together an offer, you will be informed. Stay in touch with your contact and be ready to act on a moment's notice.

Post-offer Tasks

So far, you have been concentrating on steps required to get one or preferably multiple job offers. Once you begin to receive them, you will have another set of tasks in hand. Firstly, you will have to acknowledge and keep early offers pending. Then, after you have more offers in hand, you will have to evaluate them. We take a look at these tasks.

Dealing with Early Offers

Unless the very first offer is from the best organisation, you will have to keep offers open yet pending

This situation can arise if you have applied for a number of jobs at the same time and only some interviews have taken place, while others are still in the pipeline. While you will be happy to receive an offer, you must consider the situation calmly. If you are very lucky, the offer will be from the organisation that was your first choice. This one is easy. All you do is accept the job and send the others your regrets.

However, life is rarely so simple. Often, you will want to wait for other offers. Yet, you would like to keep the offer you have received open for consideration. Here are some guidelines for dealing with such situations in a deft and skilful manner.

The Very First Step

The first thing you should do when you receive an early offer is to make other organisations immediately aware of the offer. Your stock will go up markedly the moment you get one offer in hand, since it becomes known that you have been found suitable by one of the employers. Some employers, who may have been looking at other interviewees, will now be forced to act and make you an offer. Things will begin to happen!

> ***Make sure that each potential employer knows about the offer you get***

The second thing to do is ask the organisation that made the initial offer for as much time as possible to make your decision. The amount of time you request should depend on the other pending offers. One week's lead time is common and you might be able to get as much as two weeks' time. You can now see the importance of staying in touch with each potential organisation.

> ***Seek sufficient time to evaluate competing offers***

You Will Lose Some

After your selected companies are informed about the job offer you have, do not be surprised if some of them suddenly back off because they may realise that they cannot match the offer you already have.

If your initial offer is from an industry or market leader, you may find it difficult to attract a second, matching offer. However, the very fact that others are unable or unwilling to match the offer you already have is a confirmation of its soundness and desirability.

Evaluating Multiple Job Offers

Once you have received offers from the organisations you had short-listed, it is time to compare and evaluate them. We give below the guidelines you may follow to evaluate the offers and select the best ones for subsequent salary negotiations.

Weighing All the Factors

How do you decide which job is right for you? Begin by developing a pros-and-cons list for each job. Make sure this list is comprehensive. Think about the features of each offer, such as salary, benefits, corporate culture, time needed to travel to the workplace, the organisation's track record, on-the-job learning opportunities and any other relevant factor. While listing the factors, you should err on the side of too many rather than too little. Later, you can always eliminate factors that do not show any significant difference between competing offers.

Here are some factors you may wish to consider:

- Advancement opportunities
- Amount of travel
- Benefits
- Level of autonomy
- Level of responsibility
- Location
- Market value of skills/experience that you will get from the job
- Opportunities to learn and grow in job/company
- Organisational culture
- Prestige of job or organisation
- Quality of higher management
- Salary

- Stability of industry
- Stability of organisation
- Support for continuing education or advanced degree
- Training and development opportunities

Select Relevant Factors

If you have done a SWOT analysis on yourself as recommended in Chapter 4, *Good Preparation is Half the Battle*, earlier in this book, you will have a good idea of what is important to you because it fits in with your career goals. Give higher weights to factors that are more important.

> ***Give higher ranking to factors that are more important to your career goals***

Think back to the time when you began your job search. Remind yourself of the considerations that were important to you. Recall the factors regarding the job, organisation and work environment that were on your wish list for an ideal job.

Rank the factors you want to use to compare the job offers with your modified wish list as a guide. The most important criterion in your wish list gets number one rank in your factor comparison list. The next important criterion in your wish list is given number two rank and so on. Rank all the factors in your factor comparison chart this way. Now find the organisation that scores the highest in your factor comparison chart. That is the job for you! If there is a tie, use your gut feeling!

TIP

It is a common mistake to rate the salary package as the most important criteria. Instead, look for reputation and track records of each organisation. Choose the one that displays better growth and has a corporate culture that you can fit into. In short, do not select a particular offer just because it has better pay and benefits.

Money will not be reward enough a year from now if you begin to hate your work and the work culture. Do not be afraid to listen to your gut feeling. Your instinct will be right more often than you think!

Room for Negotiation

Perhaps an offer is attractive, but there is a specific problem. In that case, it is worth exploring if there is room for finding a middle ground. Contact the organisation to set up a meeting. For instance, the job may appear ideal except that you cannot join for another month. Or, you are attending evening classes and cannot go on shift duty for another month. You may be able to negotiate a compromise on such issues.

Declining Offers Gracefully

It is advisable to have more than one offer in hand until the salary negotiations are over. However, there will be some dropouts from your list. This may happen as you evaluate offers and seek the clarifications you need. Some jobs may emerge as a poor fit as far as your career goals are concerned, or the salary package may be really out of line with other offers and the gap too large for any hope of compromise. It is time, then, to say goodbye to that offer.

TIP

Do not merely forget about the offer. Telephone or write to them, declining the offer. Keep in mind the importance of being diplomatic when rejecting an offer, because in today's fact-paced work world, you can never know when you may have to contact them again.

TOP

Here is an example of diplomatically declining an offer: "I really appreciate your offer. I find however that another position that I have been offered is a better fit for my career goals. I really want to say how impressed I am with your company and how much I have enjoyed the opportunity to meet members of your organisation. Perhaps in the future, there will be something that is a better fit for both of us."

A last word of advice—do pass on details of offers you decline to your less fortunate friends looking for jobs. Someday, they may do you a good turn as well!

8. Salary Negotiations

WHAT THIS CHAPTER CONTAINS

- Key strategies for negotiations
- Establishing a salary range
- Your magic number
- Handling premature salary enquiries
- Making the transition
- A salary quiz to test you

No! I was not fired. They
BEGGED me to leave them!

The Art of Negotiating Salary

Discussing salary with a prospective employer is a procedure that requires both tact and know-how. In this chapter, you will learn how to negotiate an attractive compensation package for yourself without offending or alienating your future employers.

When you discuss the subject of salary negotiation with your friends, they will tell you things like:

- He or she who mentions a salary figure first will lose the negotiation
- You cannot negotiate successfully without knowing your exact market value
- Suspect any employer who presses you for a quick decision

> ***The art of salary negotiation lies in converting a win-lose confrontation into a win-win strategy***

While there is some truth in each of these statements, they give you the feeling that salary negotiation is a battle between two opponents, a win-lose confrontation in which if you benefit, the organisation will lose and vice versa. It need not be so. If you have a clear understanding of the negotiation process and if you prepare thoroughly before the negotiations, you can turn the exercise into a win-win strategy in which both the organisation and you will stand to benefit.

The Key Strategy

The key to successful negotiation lies in your carefully-planned strategy involving three elements: preparation, presentation and patience. Of these, preparation is probably the single most important part. A successful trial lawyer will tell you that the key to presenting a good case in the courtroom is the hours of preparation that goes beforehand. The same is true for successful negotiations. A well researched and a well-prepared case will almost present itself! Here are some guidelines for research, preparation and practice.

Do Your Research

Gather as much factual information as you can about your current market value and compensation practices of the organisation you are negotiating with. If you have already received other offers, you will know your market value. If not, your current salary will have to do as your guide. Include any salary survey information that you have. See the section below under *Preparing a Salary Range* for more details.

> ***Be very clear about the minimum increase in pay that will justify the risk of a job change***

Be very clear about the minimum increase in pay that will justify the risk of leaving your current job for a new and potentially uncertain job. You must find out if the interviewing organisation has fixed salary grades, and what they are. If so, you will be slotted within an existing framework. If you see that the scope of the base salary package is limited, you may be able to negotiate a package of perquisites that give you tax relief or compensate you in other ways.

Psychological Preparation

It is unlikely that you will know the person with whom you will negotiate in advance. Therefore, you will not have advance knowledge about his communication style and decision-making behaviour. You will have to decide how much firmness you must display and how much accommodation you must make as the negotiation progresses. In short, you will have to observe, learn and plan your strategy as you go along. The soundness of the background information that you collect will bolster your confidence and give teeth to your arguments.

Be sure you know exactly what you want as your compensation package, not just the approximate amount of your salary, but the whole package including perquisites. While this does not mean that you will get everything you want, having the information clear in your head will help you determine to what extent you can concede and where you

> ***Be sure that you know exactly what you want as a compensation package***

must draw the line. If you know exactly where you must stop, your manner will convey your determination to the interviewer. Bargaining will usually stop when the interviewer can see that your limit has been reached.

Practise

Rehearse the presentation of your case. Describe and justify the compensation you expect, using a friend to act the part of the employer. If you make mistakes in this rehearsal, you will get a chance to correct your mistakes without harming the actual negotiations. Ask your friend to criticise your presentation and analyse your reasoning. This will help you prepare for questions you should expect and pitfalls you should avoid. If all this seems a lot of work, remember that if something is worth negotiating for, it is also worth preparing for.

Beginning Negotiations

When you begin, put aside the issue of compensation and focus on the content and future of the job. After you have decided that the job is right for you, then focus on the compensation package.

Desired Salary for the Job

Although salary is usually discussed only when you are being seriously considered, most job applications will ask you to fill in a 'desired salary' amount. When you fill in the job application, do not give a specific figure for 'desired salary'. Instead, use one of the following two lines:

- Open to negotiations
- Seeking a competitive salary

You do not wish to be tied down to a number at this stage before you know what the employer is willing to pay you. If the job is really what you want, you do not wish to be dropped from consideration because you have quoted too high a figure. Conversely, the job may be worth much more than the figure you have mentioned. If

> ***By quoting a specific figure at the start of negotiations, you place yourself at a relative disadvantage***

so, you leave yourself no room to negotiate further. Either way, by quoting a specific figure, you will place yourself at a disadvantage. Wait for the actual negotiations to begin before committing yourself. In the meanwhile, well before the negotiations begin, you must get your facts together.

Later in this chapter, we will discuss how you can fend off premature questions on your salary expectations.

Preparing a Salary Range

Come to the negotiation table armed with clear information about what you must get as a compensation package before you make a career move. If this is your first job, you should work out a 'reserve price' for yourself, below which you would rather wait for the next offer. If you are changing jobs, put a price for the risk you will take in making a job change. In either case, establish a personal salary range. To do so, here is what you need to know:

Minimum Salary: Determine the minimum amount of money for which you will accept this job offer. Do not disclose this figure, but keep it at the back of your mind.

Market Price Range: Find out what a person with your skills is worth in the marketplace. The following list highlights good sources for this information:

- Professional journals
- Magazines, newspapers, etc
- Executive search professionals or headhunters
- Peers and colleagues
- National salary surveys
- Other job offers

Dream Salary Figure: Determine a figure that would really be your dream come true. You can select the top of the market price range as this figure. This is your starting number for salary negotiations. Remember it is easy to lower your original figure, but it is almost impossible to raise it.

Your minimum salary requirement and your market value determine the low end of your salary range. Your dream salary determines the top end of your salary range. Be sure that your range is realistic, based on the market price of the special knowledge and the years of experience that you bring to the employer.

Consider other forms of compensation that may play a role in the total package. Determine what each is worth to you. Here are some of the main components that go into a salary package:

- Annual bonus
- Base salary
- Company car or car allowance and other forms of travel compensation
- Coverage of dependants in medical insurance schemes
- Earned leave, casual leave and medical leave
- Gratuity and provident funds
- Medical benefits
- Performance or profit-sharing bonus
- Retirement or pension plans
- Stock option or stock purchase plans for employees

For many organisations, year-end bonuses or a Diwali bonus are a common part of total compensation. Ask about past bonus levels and get estimates on future performance. As a general rule, bonuses are not guaranteed, so make sure you understand the conditions for receiving them. Determine if bonuses are based on personal, departmental or company-wide performance. Similarly, enquire into the qualifying criteria for gratuity and provident fund schemes as well.

Strategy During Negotiations

Reaching Your Magic Number

Always discuss salary in person, not over the phone. It is much easier to read the persons opposite you when you can see their faces and interpret their body language. Remember, companies are responsible for acquiring your services at a reasonable price to them. On the other hand, negotiating the best deal for yourself is your sole responsibility. Do not be afraid to bargain hard. Companies regard people with good negotiating skills as a valuable asset to their firm since, as an employee, you can use the same skills on behalf of your employer!

Do not bargain hard just for the sake of appearing to be a tough negotiator

However, be reasonable. You should not be seen to bargain hard just for the sake of appearing to be a tough negotiator. Be willing to adjust your expectations based on your market value. At the same time, do not accept an offer that does not make you happy. Accepting an underpaid job will serve neither you nor the company in the long run. Nobody wants to be, or engage, an unhappy employee.

Respond to queries about salary expectations by providing full details of your current salary

It is important to get the employer to offer the first concrete number. When an employer asks questions such as, "How much will you expect to join us?" or "What are your salary expectations or requirements?" do not provide a specific figure. We have already discussed the disadvantage of doing so. Instead, respond by laying out the details of your current compensation package. Give a detailed basic salary and perquisites breakdown. Discuss other forms of compensation that you currently receive, including any special allowances, stock options, medical benefits, etc. State that you are open to a good counter-offer. More strategies to handle premature salary questions are discussed later in this chapter.

In the next discussion with the employer, begin by listing parts of the compensation package that both agree to, so that the discussion starts on a note of agreement. Then suggest an increase in the base salary or the perquisites. If you have a good track record of past success in similar jobs, use that as a justification for a higher starting salary. If the proposed compensation package does not include a perquisite you currently get, that will be what you should point out. Conclude your presentation with a counter-question: "What figure do you feel is appropriate for someone with my skills?"

> ***In the second round, begin by listing areas of agreement first. Then suggest reasons why you should be paid more than the offer on the table***

If the revised offer is acceptable, consider accepting on the spot. Many companies give their best offer in the first or the second round and will not negotiate any further. It is vital to interpret the mood and body language of the negotiator of the organisation. If you misread the signs and try to push the bargaining process too far, you will not get the job.

TIP

Handling Premature Salary Enquiries

Salary negotiation is something that hiring managers do for a living. They are therefore a lot better at it than the candidates. To have a better chance against these professionals, it is necessary to devote enough time to perfect your technique, especially the skills to handle premature salary questions that you will surely be asked.

To reduce employee costs, almost all companies play a nasty little game. They ask you how much you want. You will see a specific entry in a company application form that asks you to indicate your desired salary. Most of the time, you tend to automatically fill in all blanks on a form. So, you put down a figure. As we have already discussed under *Preliminary Negotiations* earlier in this chapter, use one of the suggested answers instead of a figure. If you have done your research well, you will have a minimum acceptable salary in your head. Leave it there; do not put it down in the form!

Since you have not indicated a figure in your application form, you will be asked for a figure during the interview. Here is a step-by-step approach to the question-and-answer session that will follow:

TOP

Step 1: The first time they ask you how much you expect, reply: "I am much more interested in an organisation like yours and in meeting the challenges of the job than I am in the size of the initial offer."

This sentence is constructed with great care. You may want to memorise it. It does several things for you. It is excellent public relations. The vast majority of people answer the salary question with a number. However, unlike the rest, you focus on the job and not the compensation. Thereby, you will instantly distinguish yourself from the competition. You will also avoid answering their question.

In four cases out of ten, this is all you need to say. The interviewer will look up your current earnings and make you a fair offer. However, in the remaining six cases, they will ask you again. If they do, go to Step 2.

TOP

Step 2: The second time they ask, reply: "I will consider any reasonable offer."

This is basically a stalling tactic. The word "consider" will give you a lot of leeway. Add to it the various interpretations possible of the word "reasonable". Taken together, you will see that the sentence has no real meaning at all. However, you have been polite and, once more, you have avoided naming the salary figure first!

Only very determined employers will still insist that you name your salary expectations first. If that happens, go to Step 3.

TOP

Step 3: The third time they ask, reply: "You are in a much better position to know how much I am worth to you than I am."

Once again, you have been polite and, again, you have refused to put down a figure. You have also told them, in so many words, that you have seen through their little game. Any employer who seriously wants to offer you a job will surely make you an offer now, opening the way for you to use all your research information and negotiating skills to your best advantage. If no offer materialises after this, the employer is not serious. You will do well to look elsewhere!

After Negotiations

Making the Transition

Once you have made your decision, accept the job verbally. Restate the terms of the offer to spell out exactly what you are accepting. Inform them that you will resign after receiving a written offer from them. Inform them of the minimum time you will need to join them. The time will depend mainly on the notice period that you are obliged to give your present employer.

TIP

Get the offer in writing. Be sure that it includes your start date, salary, perquisites, job title, benefits and any other items promised. Write your resignation letter and present it to your current employers only after receiving a written offer. Inform your new employers as soon as you have handed in your resignation letter.

You should call each of your interviewers to thank them for their role in the process and express your desire to join the firm as soon as you are released. While you are on the phone with them, ask them if there is anything you can do, in advance, to help speed up your integration into the new work environment.

Counter-offers

Your current employer will often extend a counter-offer after you have resigned. This is very likely if you work in a specialised, difficult-to-replace job. In addition, there are a number of reasons why your present employer may not want to let you go. These include:

- It is cheaper to give you a raise than it would be to recruit a new employee.

- Companies do not want sensitive or confidential information going to a competitor.
- Companies do not want skilled professionals going to competitors.
- The project you were working on will suffer delays because of your departure.
- Companies want to have low turnover rate.

TRAP

You will be given some of these reasons and also promised a tempting salary package. However, our advice to you is not to accept a counter-offer. We list some of the reasons why you should not stay after resigning:

- While you may get more money, your original reasons for wishing to leave your job will still remain.
- The extra money offered will probably come out of your next increment or bonus!
- Your loyalty to the company will always be suspect in future. When the next promotion time comes around, managers remember who was loyal and who was not.

It has been found that almost 80% of all employees who accept the present employer's counter-offer leave within six months to a year anyway.

Salary Quiz

We have now covered the theoretical aspects and many practical techniques required for successful salary negotiations. By the time you have read through this chapter, you should feel confident of handling your own salary negotiations. As we have already said, a great deal of your success will depend on the depth and quality of your preparations.

Test how ready you are to tackle the real thing by answering the dozen questions given below. It will tell you what you know (or do not know) about negotiating your salary.

Directions

There are 12 questions in this quiz. Each may be answered as **True**, **False** or **Don't Know** by ticking the appropriate box. Correct answers will be found at the end of the quiz. There is no time limit for taking the test.

Questions

1) Salary negotiations affect not only your pay, but your performance on the job as well.

☐ True ☐ False ☐ Don't Know

2) If the employer's offer is significantly higher than your market value, you should accept it and get it in writing right away.

☐ True ☐ False ☐ Don't Know

3) Employers will often calculate a salary offer to you as a percentage increase over your present earnings. To make the interview process go smoothly, get the expected percentage agreed at the beginning of the interview.

☐ True ☐ False ☐ Don't Know

4) Avoid interview calls for jobs where the salary is significantly below your expectations because it wastes both your time and that of the interviewers.

☐ True ☐ False ☐ Don't Know

5) At the time of final negotiations, you should start with a number that is at the high end of your range; that way you will have room to negotiate.

☐ True ☐ False ☐ Don't Know

6) Good benefits will not make up for a poor base salary.

☐ True ☐ False ☐ Don't Know

7) To find your fair market value, you have only to find out what others in similar positions are earning.

☐ True ☐ False ☐ Don't Know

8) Straight commission is the riskiest type of compensation, although you might have to accept it if you are inexperienced in the sales of that particular line of products.

☐ True ☐ False ☐ Don't Know

9) An average wage earner would add an additional Rs 10 lakhs to his career earnings if his salary negotiation skills increased his income by just ten percent.

☐ True ☐ False ☐ Don't Know

10) You should disclose your current compensation during salary negotiations in complete detail, even corroborating earnings with your current salary slip if asked for.

☐ True ☐ False ☐ Don't Know

11) One acceptable way to increase your negotiation advantage is to inflate the amount of your present earnings when you negotiate. Therefore, you should add 10% to your base salary to cover benefits, and add any anticipated bonus or expected pay increase when you give the employer your current income.

☐ True ☐ False ☐ Don't Know

12) Any one of these questions that you answered incorrectly could easily cost you thousands of rupees in actual salary negotiations.

☐ True ☐ False ☐ Don't Know

Answers to Salary Quiz

1) **True**. A poorly negotiated salary will adversely affect your attitude at work. The poor attitude will eventually affect your performance and your chances for raises or promotions.

2) **False**. If you are overpaid, you should find out why. If it is a mistake, it will not last. On the other hand, if there is a hidden sinister reason, you should get out, fast!

3) **False**. Although most employers will like to know your current salary because they want to be sure that they can make you an attractive offer, you need not disclose your expectations at too early a stage. By doing so, you run the risk of over- or under-valuing yourself and thus lose your bargaining advantage.

4) **False**. While you should not take interviews for fun, each interview is an opportunity to hone your negotiating skills. You cannot know in advance what opportunities may open up even from what looks like an unpromising offer at first glance. Therefore, do not give up an opportunity.

5) **False**. You should not be talked into being the first to indicate a figure for your salary.

6) **False**. There are many combinations of benefits and perquisites that can make the whole package acceptable, even when the base salary is low.

7) **False**. There are three components that determine your fair market value. These are – your current salary, the going market rate and the skills and knowledge that you will bring to the job.

8) **False**. Straight commission is the safest kind of compensation. It is acceptable in many situations, regardless of your experience level.

9) **True**. Ten percent increase in earnings spread over a career lifetime of 30 to 35 years will often add up to over Rs 10 lakhs!

10) **True**. Being straightforward will generally work in your favour. Remember that the interviewing company can always verify this figure after you have joined them. If your current income is much lower than the market rate, you will have to overcome this drawback by convincing the new employers of your true worth.

11) **False**. Inflating your earnings is a bad idea. It has all sorts of potential dangers. The best strategy is to avoid discussion of your earnings at all until there is an offer. See the previous section for a step-by-step procedure to handle premature enquiries about your salary expectations.

12) **True**. Any wrong answer could easily cost you thousands. We hope you have had fun taking the quiz and getting the point!

9. Frequently Asked Questions

WHAT THIS CHAPTER CONTAINS

- ➢ Examples of common questions you can expect
- ➢ The three key questions employers ask
- ➢ Standard questions for practising your answers
- ➢ Complex questions and top answer

Then for the next 25 years I held the same job. All my friends told me that they had never seen such determination!

JLN

Practising Answers

In this chapter, as part of your preparation for succeeding in the interview, we will help you practise giving the right answers to a variety of questions. It is surprising how little time most candidates spend in preparation. Although you would have spent several years to acquire your impressive qualifications and wide-ranging experience, when the time comes to showcase all your accomplishments and skills, you will probably spend more time in writing your résumé than preparing effective answers to the interviewer's questions!

In any job interview, there is a set of common questions that almost all interviewers will ask you in one form or another. The questions will relate to your education, experience, knowledge, skills and attitudes. We have prepared a list of basic questions that cover almost all the variants you are likely to face. Practise answering these questions based on the facts of your own case and you will be able to reply convincingly and confidently. However, so will all the other good candidates competing with you for the job! That is why you have to prepare answers to difficult questions as well.

There is a set of common questions that almost all interviewers ask

TIP

You must expect some difficult questions to come your way. Questions that will catch you off guard and make you stumble, hesitate and stutter. Remember that it is how you deal with these difficult questions that will set you apart and ultimately determine your success or failure.

For example, the interviewer may ask you: "What is the worst thing you have heard about our company?"

He may then follow with another question: "I am still not really sure if you are suitable for this job. What do you think?"

One or two more questions like these and soon everything becomes a haze and before you know it the interview is over. Needless to say, your

Handling difficult questions is a matter of learning and you can master it too

performance has been far from satisfactory. Sounds intimidating? Perhaps, but remember that handling questions like these is not really difficult. It is just a matter of learning a skill and you can learn to do so with a little effort and help from this book.

TIP

This skill of coping with awkward questions is something you will need all your life. In today's fast-changing world, most of us will change jobs up to 10 times in our career. Every time you appear for an interview, you will need this skill to see you through. Even if you do not change jobs so often, you will still need this skill whenever you face a promotion interview. There is indeed no escape from it!

The Key to Success

Even though we do know that answering difficult questions well is the key to success, many of us have a fatalistic attitude towards interview preparation. You may think that there are so many possible questions you could be asked that it is impossible to prepare for all of them. The possibilities are so vast that the exercise is futile. You can only hope for the best and any preparation is a waste of time.

This is a fatal mistake. The secret of success at interviews is very simple if you realise that there are only so many core questions and variations of the same basic questions that the interviewer can ask you. We have done all the hard work for you. In the second part of this chapter, we have brought together key questions that need careful answers. We have grouped the questions under different sub-headings for easy reference and we have given you an ordinary answer, a top-quality answer and explained why the latter is top quality.

You need not commit top answers to memory, only understand the logic

Best of all, you need not try to commit the questions and answers to memory. What you need to do instead is to thoroughly understand the principles that make the top answers outstanding. Once you have mastered the underlying principles, you will be able to answer other difficult questions on your own, producing convincing, logical and impressive answers each time.

When you read through each question and its two answers, do pay attention to the explanatory note after each top answer. The note will help you fully understand each question, the real implication behind the question and the strategy used in the top answer to deal with it.

After you have read this chapter and practised your question-answer session, your answers will have an impact on the interviewer. They will have a power, a force and a sharpness that will carry real conviction. They will create an impression of you as an intelligent, decisive person, someone who remains calm and poised no matter what is thrown at him or her. You will also feel more relaxed and confident about your interview, as you will be well prepared for any unexpected surprises.

Standard Questions

Employers may ask you a variety of questions but, in essence, apart from the salary you expect, they only want to know three things, and these are the questions you need to answer with some evidence to back up your claims. The questions are:

1. "Can you do the job?"

Do you have the appropriate qualifications, knowledge, skills and experience to do what they want you to?

2. "Will you do the job?"

Do you have the right motivation and enthusiasm? Are you really keen on this job or would you rather be doing something else? If you enjoy the job, you will work hard and they will get value for money.

3. "Will you fit in?"

Do you fit in with the people who work there? Would people enjoy working with you or would you seriously damage the morale of others around you?

We have prepared a fairly exhaustive list of questions based on these themes, arranged under appropriate sub-headings for your convenience. Read them and practise answers to them based on your own résumé.

List of Questions

About You

- Will you give me an idea of your background in your area of specialisation?
- Tell me about yourself.
- What prompted you to apply for this position?
- What are you good at doing? What do you dislike doing?
- How do you get along with different kinds of people?
- What are your goals? What are you doing to achieve these goals?
- What do you hope to be doing in 5 years, 10 years or 20 years?
- What kinds of things worry you?
- Tell me about the last time you were angry at work.
- How did your previous employer get the best out of you?
- Are you interested in sports?
- Do you prefer working with others or alone?
- What sets you apart from other candidates?
- When do you expect a promotion?
- Who are your heroes? What do you admire most? Why?

About Your Attitudes

- What do you look for in a job?
- What frustrated you in your previous job?
- What was your single most important contribution in your last job?
- If you could create a job for yourself, what would it be?
- How do you feel about travel and/or relocation?

About Your Attitude to Problems

- Suppose you ran into a problem with your colleagues. How would you handle it?
- Tell me about a situation that really challenged you and how you met the challenge.
- What kinds of decisions are most difficult for you?
- Are you willing to take calculated risks when necessary?
- What problem are you most proud of having solved? How did it benefit your company?

About Your Approach to the Boss

- What are your boss's responsibilities?
- Tell me about your best boss?
- What did you learn from your boss?
- Do you prefer to work for one who delegates or one who supervises you closely?
- What approach works best to get the most out of you?

About Your Career

- What are your future career plans? Why did you choose your particular career?
- What qualifications do you have that make you feel you would be successful in your field?
- What are the disadvantages of your chosen field?
- What do you know about opportunities in the field in which you are trained?
- What do you think determines a person's progress in a good company?
- Do you prefer any specific geographic location? Why?
- Do you prefer to work in a large or small city?
- Do you like to work for a large or a small company?

About Your Education

- In what school activities have you participated? Why? Which ones did you enjoy the most?
- What courses did you like best? Least? Why?
- Do you consider your education valuable? Why?
- How did you spend your vacations while in college?
- Do you think your extra-curricular activities were worth the time? Why?
- Have you ever changed your major field of interest while studying? Why?
- Do you feel you have done the best scholastic work of which you are capable?
- Have you ever had any difficulty getting along with fellow students and teachers?

About Former Employment

- What jobs have you held? How were they obtained, and why did you leave?
- What do you think of your previous employer?
- Will your previous employer recommend you?
- What have you learned from the jobs you have held?
- What jobs have you enjoyed the most? The least? Why?
- Have you ever trained anyone to do a job?
- Did you train your replacement?

About the Interviewing Company

- Why do you want to work for our company?
- What do you know about our company?
- What interests you about our product or service?

About Salary Expectations

- What are your ideas on salary?
- What salary do you expect on this job?
- How much did you get in your last job?
- Would you be willing to work for the minimum wage in our salary range?

About Your Personal Life

- What types of books have you read?
- Do you enjoy sports as a participant? As a spectator?
- What do you do to keep in good physical condition?
- Have you ever had any serious illness or injury?

About Self-evaluation

- Are you mainly interested in money or do you feel that your career is more important?
- Can you take instructions without feeling upset?
- Do you like routine work?
- Do you like regular hours?
- What is your major weakness?
- Define cooperation.
- Will you fight to get ahead?
- Do you demand attention?
- Do you have an analytical mind?
- Are you eager to please?
- Is it an effort for you to be tolerant of persons with a background and interest different from your own?
- What are your own special abilities? Strengths?
- Do you like to travel?

- How about overtime work?
- What have you done which shows initiative and willingness to work?
- Define success.

Comments: Many of the questions in the list given above do not contain any hidden pitfalls. However, to be convincing and effective, you must prepare your answers in advance.

TIP

Firstly, you must back up claims of good performance with examples from your job history. Secondly, you must take every possible opportunity to highlight a good fit between your capabilities and the job needs. Practise these replies and wait for the right opportunity to bring up instances of good performance and good matches during the interview. Notice how much more convincing and impressive your answers will be with a little prior practice.

Additional Tips

Here are some general tips you may wish to keep in mind when preparing your answers:

- Most employers are not formally trained interviewers. Be prepared with some well thought out answers so that you come across as a competent professional.
- Keep your responses focused on the question and the employer's needs. You will be surprised at how many candidates say too much or go off on tangents during an interview. All they succeed in doing is reveal negative or controversial things about themselves.
- Avoid talking negatively about past jobs and co-workers. Stay clear of personal problems or bias. Focus on your desire to be an asset to anyone hiring your skills.

Complex Questions

So far, we have looked at fairly routine questions. However, during interviews, you will come across questions that require a bit of thought before you answer them. The interviewer may ask them with the deliberate intention of gauging your reaction to a tricky question, or because he wishes to probe further.

Any probing or provoking question you get will require some thought and preparation on your part. You may consider these questions irritating or threatening. However, they also give you an opportunity to perform better than the competition. It is the well thought out answer to a difficult question that will make you stand out from others.

> ***A well thought out answer to a difficult question will make you stand out***

Now we look at these difficult questions, each with one ordinary and one top answer, along with explanatory comments. The questions are grouped together under several appropriate sub-headings for your convenience.

TRAP

A word of caution is appropriate here. It is very unlikely that your own education, job history or background will match each top answer. Do not attempt to make up your answer just to sound impressive. Apart from the poor ethics involved, think of the damage to your career if you are exposed.

Instead, concentrate on the reasoning that makes an answer a top one. Once you have understood the underlying logic, you will be able to modify the top answers given here to fit your own case. Then your answers will be correct, applicable to you and yet carry a winning punch!

Filling in the Gaps

If your job history has gaps, it is sure to raise questions.

Question: Your résumé does not say what you were doing between July 1998 and April 1999.

Ordinary Answer: Sorry! I was looking for a job then.

Top Answer: I took a part-time job and an evening course on computer programming.

Comments: In both cases, the candidate was obviously looking for a job. However, in the second case, the candidate did something useful while waiting. The part-time job was probably to pay for the course.

Relating Past Behaviour to Future Performance

Through these questions, the interviewer attempts to predict future behaviour based on your past performance.

Question: Why did you decide to learn using computers after getting your degree?

Ordinary Answer: All my friends were doing the same thing.

Top Answer: I was fortunate. My father bought me a computer. I became familiar and proficient and I could see a future for me in the software industry.

Comments: The ordinary response indicates a passive, unambitious candidate, whereas the top answer indicates someone with well thought out, long-term commitment to his profession.

Question: How did you get along with your last boss?

Ordinary Answer: Nothing special happened.

Top Answer: Most stimulating, including our differences. I have learned a great deal about managing people from him.

Comments: The ordinary answer sounds a little evasive. The top answer is honest, indicating that they did not always agree. However, the candidate took it all correctly, as a good learning experience.

Question: What was your outstanding achievement in the last job?

Ordinary Answer: There were many highlights. Nothing very specific. In a recessive market, just keeping the job going was an achievement in itself.

TOP

Top Answer: The launch of our new brand of soap in Chennai. In two years, we captured 35% of the market and became the brand leader.

Comments: The ordinary answer appears to have been thought up on the spot, while the top answer is specific, quantified and focussed.

Professional and Technical Competence

The interviewer tries to assess how well qualified you are for the job.

Question: Since graduation, what have you done to keep your knowledge up to date?

Ordinary Answer: Little outside my job. But the job itself is an excellent teacher.

TOP

Top Answer: I have taken courses in public speaking and management skills.

Comments: The ordinary answer shows no initiative. The top answer is specific and shows long-term career planning.

Question: In your career so far, what are the three most important skills you have learned?

Ordinary Answer: Job knowledge, how to get along with people and teamwork.

TOP

Top Answer: I have become computer literate, I have learned how to sell ideas to my colleagues and boss and I have carefully studied the work style of my boss in preparation for a likely promotion.

Comments: The ordinary answer says what anyone would

learn on the job. There is no evidence of effort. The top job shows clear career planning and equally clear goals for advancement.

Scope and Responsibilities of Last Job

Your suitability is being assessed by examining the scope of your last job and the responsibilities that you carried.

TOP

Question: Tell me about a recent project you handled and explain what aspects gave you the most satisfaction.

Ordinary Answer: There were some relatively small projects. Unfortunately, my job had limited authority.

Top Answer: I changed the tendering system for office supplies. While there was some initial resistance, ultimately the new system worked well and we saved over Rs 2 lakhs annually.

Comments: The ordinary answer may be honest, but it is typical of someone used to complaining rather than making things happen. The top answer is precise and the benefit has been quantified.

Question: Why do you want to leave your current job?

Ordinary Answer: I have been at my present job for three years. It is time to move on.

TOP

Top Answer: I have been quite happy in my current job and I was not looking actively for a change. However, your offer will really allow my capabilities to be stretched. It is the next logical step in my career.

Comments: The ordinary answer has nothing positive in it and may even hint at stagnation. The top answer on the other hand indicates a very good candidate with clear career goals.

Matching Your Skills with the Job

The interviewer has already formed an opinion of your suitability based on your résumé. He is now getting more details and supporting information from you.

Question: Why have you applied for this job?

Ordinary Answer: My present job gives me no chance to use my education and skills. I have a lot more to offer and I am looking for a chance to do so.

TOP

Top Answer: From the advertisement and my enquiries in the market, this job fits in well with my skills and past experience. You have an excellent reputation already and my marketing skills can surely help make the product a market leader.

Comments: The ordinary answer may, at first glance, sound impressive. However, the candidate has said nothing except that he is unhappy. On the other hand, the top answer is specific. It is a clear statement how the organisation can benefit by hiring the candidate.

Question: What special skills can you bring to this job that will benefit the organisation?

Ordinary Answer: I have years of experience. I am used to all aspects of your manufacturing process due to my experience in similar organisations.

TOP

Top Answer: I know about polymers both from my chemical engineering degree and my three years in Reliance Industries. I develop and assist vendors in my present job and have first-hand experience in guiding their quality control departments and in solving their problems.

Comments: The ordinary answer says nothing specific, perhaps because the candidate has done nothing outstanding. The top answer, on the other hand, is clearly that of a qualified achiever with valuable field experience.

Salary Expectations

TRAP

If you are faced with these questions before you have an offer in hand, be careful that you do not commit yourself into a non-bargainable position. The interviewer will, of course, try to pin you down to a figure that you cannot exceed later.

Question: You know of our usual policy of giving you a small increase over your current salary. Are you ready to accept?

Ordinary Answer: I have not really thought about that. However, I am sure that salary will not be a problem.

TOP

Top Answer: Salary is not the most important thing for me. Job satisfaction and growth opportunity is much more important. However, a job change does include a risk and, therefore, deserves a suitable increase. As we explore my suitability for the job, I am sure you will be able to suggest an appropriate compensation for me.

Comments: The ordinary answer is too casual. It may even imply that you are open to almost any offer. In the top answer, you have indicated that a small increase is not enough, but have kept the door open for negotiation.

Outside Interests

The interviewer wants to know about your activities outside the job. On the one hand, he is looking for evidence of community involvement and leadership. On the other hand, he is trying to find out if your outside commitments will interfere with the job.

Question: I see from your résumé that you enjoy reading. What is the last book you have read?

Ordinary Answer: It is hard to remember. I read quite a bit, mostly business magazines.

TOP

Top Answer: I have been reading the *Global Manager* by XYZ lately. I do believe that the impact of globalisation is now quite widespread in India. Already a number of Indian companies are expanding abroad through acquisitions or mergers. I think the new Indian manager will need a global mindset.

Comments: The ordinary answer makes you wonder if the candidate ventures beyond the TV guide and pulp fiction. The top answer shows a better understanding of the environment.

Question: I see that you are the secretary of your drama society. Since this job will frequently send you out of town, how will the society get by?

Ordinary Answer: I am sure they will get by without me. My job comes first!

TOP

Top Answer: We work as a team. Others will pitch in. Another member will be made secretary. I shall still be able to guide and contribute whenever I can.

Comments: The ordinary answer appears to be framed just to please the prospective employers. There is a hint of indifference to the society in spite of the candidate being the secretary, which is not a healthy attitude. In comparison, the top response is practical, and shows that the candidate has thought out how to transfer the responsibility in an orderly manner.

Self-image

A candidate's image of himself is a valuable indicator of his personality. The interviewer can judge your maturity and mental balance by listening to how you describe yourself.

Question: How will your closest friends describe you?

Ordinary Answer: I have never asked for my friends' opinions.

TOP

Top Answer: I can think of them mentioning traits like reliable, intelligent and a finisher who does get things done in the end.

Comments: A person who has no idea of what his best friends think of him is either exceptionally insensitive or very conceited. The top answer sounds plausible, although the candidate may be voicing his own opinion.

Question: What makes you really angry?

Ordinary Answer: The usual things, long queues, endless waits, uncalled for insults and the like.

TOP

Top Answer: I am usually quite calm. Losing one's temper is about the worst way of getting what you want.

Comments: The ordinary answer merely shows very human impatience. The top answer shows maturity and the patience required to make things happen in the real world.

Career Planning

Question: How will your move to this job fit in with your long-term career plans?

Ordinary Answer: It will be a good step upwards and in the right direction.

TOP

Top Answer: It will provide the practical experience I need to add to my theoretical knowledge in computer science. The opportunity to work as a team leader of a software development group is exactly the kind of experience I need towards becoming an IT head in the next three years.

Comments: The ordinary answer fits any candidate for any job. It does not indicate conscious career planning. The top answer, on the other hand, is specific and well thought out. The candidate can clearly see his career goal and knows that he is taking the right step.

Question: If you get this job, how long do you expect to stay with us?

Ordinary Answer: This is very difficult to say. I hope that we will develop a good working relationship and I will stay here for many years.

Top Answer: I am a steady sort of person. I do not like changing jobs as far as possible. If the challenges are as great as I feel from this interview and I make good progress in the organisation, it should be a long-term commitment.

Comments: The ordinary answer is unconvincing and non-committal. On the other hand, the top answer is reassuring to an employer. It carries conviction and rings true.

Question: If you get this job, do you intend to enhance your knowledge and skills by taking additional part-time study courses? If so, what courses do you have in mind?

Ordinary Answer: I think I will learn enough directly on the job. It will probably take up all my time.

Top Answer: In this field of customised software development, I should strengthen my knowledge of structured programming. In three years or so, I should take a course in advanced software design to qualify myself as a project leader.

Comments: The ordinary answer is that of a pedestrian performer content to do just enough. The top answer indicates that the candidate has a clearly thought out plan for progressing in knowledge and job responsibility.

Final Thoughts

We believe that the two lists, the standard questions followed by the difficult questions and their model answers together will provide you with one of the finest means of training for an interview. Practise till you are perfect and fear no interview thereafter!

10. Pitfalls to Avoid

WHAT THIS CHAPTER CONTAINS

- Why people fail in interviews
- Common but major errors
- Questions you should never ask
- Turning weaknesses into strengths

No! The boss does NOT have an eligible daughter!

Why People Fail in Interviews

Introduction

This chapter is a short overview of the mistakes and pitfalls that you must avoid in order to succeed in interviews. You have already come across many examples of mistakes to avoid in this book. Here is a comprehensive listing of what usually goes wrong in an interview and how to guard against them.

We look at errors of behaviour, of appearance or the error of asking the wrong question at the wrong time. We alert you to these so that you may check them before they happen, since slips like these may seriously damage your chances of success. We also show you how to convert some common weaknesses in your education or job history into strengths.

Common but Major Errors

Here are some of the common errors candidates make:

- Arrive late for the interview.
- Look dishevelled and inappropriately dressed.
- Adapt a bad posture and slouch in the seat.
- Fail to maintain good eye contact with the interviewer without trying to stare the interviewer down.
- Be uninformed about the organisation interviewing you.
- In your presentation, fail to make a connection between your skills and the needs of the employer.
- Speak of many accomplishments but fail to provide any quantified evidence of your achievements.
- Answer questions in an unfocused, disorganised, and rambling manner.
- Remain uninspiring and display no enthusiasm for the job.

- Answer most questions with simple "yes" and "no" without elaboration, explanation and examples required to carry conviction.
- Appear desperate for the job.
- Give obviously memorised responses, halting often and forgetting parts of what you want to say.
- Malign your current or former bosses and colleagues.
- When asked: "Do you have any questions?" reply "No."

Throughout this book, we have discussed hints, tips and advice on how to avoid these errors. Use this list to make sure you know what you should and should not do.

Questions You Should Never Ask

Here are some deadly questions that you should never ask. Asking them is the same as killing all your career opportunities with the interviewing organisation. We explain why these questions are so deadly.

What is my salary?

Do not ask about salary until the interviewer has raised the subject first. This may not happen until the second interview or even later when an offer is extended. As curious as you may be, you must be patient or risk leaving the impression that you are more interested in money than what you can contribute to the organisation.

How much earned leave and sick leave will I get?

Asking about these issues makes you seem as if you are asking for time off even before you have started on the job. Some interviewers may perceive this as a sign of lack of dedication, however unfair it may appear to you.

TIP

It is understandable that you would like to get this information. However, the best way to do so is by asking for a copy of the personnel manual, by talking to the personnel department, or by speaking with other employees before taking the job. You will be briefed on benefits at the appropriate time. If that does not happen then just ask, "What about the benefits?" But only after the salary issue has been raised.

How big is my office?

A dedicated employee and a keen team player will produce good work regardless of the office environment. Questions regarding office size may be seen as a concern about ego and appearances rather than the essential elements of the job. Usually, during a tour of the operation, you will be shown the area where you will work. There is no need to ask a pointed question regarding this.

When will I be promoted?

This question is impossible for the employer to answer. Promotion depends on your performance, openings available and the organisation's performance. Your suitability for promotion depends on your own performance together with your abilities to plan, organise and get others to perform. Questions regarding promotion should be concerned with the opportunities for advancement, rather than seeking a commitment that the employer cannot give.

Turning Weaknesses into Strengths

Evaluate negative aspects of your résumé (limited education, experience or skills; long-term absence from workforce; many jobs within a short time) and develop positive responses to questions about them.

Go back to the findings of your SWOT analysis. Look especially for shortcomings in the area of nervousness and body language. Brush up on the areas that need improvement. See Chapter 4, *Good Preparation is Half the Battle*, for more on overcoming nervousness. In the same chapter, you will find practical tips for overcoming your conscious or unconscious negative body language.

Here are some examples of how to turn around weaknesses into strengths in your résumé. You should modify the examples to suit your specific case.

Poor Academic Performance

Emphasise your excellent track record. Acknowledge that you had realised your less-than-perfect academic record and had compensated by exemplary performance on the job. If you have subsequently attended short-term courses to enhance your theoretical knowledge, such as programmes run by productivity councils or other institutions, this is the time to refer to them.

TOP

Do emphasise that you have overcome your academic shortcomings through diligent and dedicated performance. However, do not belittle academic achievement as being "too theoretical", or "not applicable to ground realities in India".

Limited Academic Achievement

Your approach is the same as in the previous case. If financial reasons prevented you from pursuing higher studies, but you did not let your performance on the job be affected as a result, you will have a persuasive argument for convincing the interviewer of your worth. If you have subsequently joined professional bodies to improve your academic standing, then limited academic achievements will not stand in your way.

Gaps in Job History

This is quite a serious drawback in your résumé. Perhaps the worst reason for a long gap is that you were waiting for the "right" job to come along. If you say so in these very words, it indicates that you have not tried hard enough or that you are difficult to satisfy. On the other hand, if you have spent the time trying to work on your own, you may have a better justification.

Be aware that employers are quite accustomed to being given "self-employment" as a reason for job history gaps. So, be prepared for a number of probing questions to follow.

TRAP

It is generally a poor strategy to invent "self-employment". Instead try to remember if you were doing a part-time job or taking some short-term course to further your career. If so, by mentioning them, you will throw more favourable light on the gaps in your employment history.

Instances of Job Severance

Job severance can be checked back by referring to your ex-employer. Therefore, complete honesty is really the best policy. If the reason is company closure or downsizing, you should not hesitate to put the facts on the table yourself. To be found out later will be disastrous for your chances of success in the new job.

11. A Bonus for You

WHAT THIS CHAPTER CONTAINS

- The nuts and bolts of résumé writing
- What type of résumé is best for you?
- A step-by-step approach to résumé writing
- Rate your résumé for content and appearance
- Further reading

This is only a short summary. The full version is in a truck parked outside your office building!

JLN

Writing Your Résumé

Not all résumés require a very high level of creativity or startling originality of approach in either their content or form. There are many conservative organisations looking for entry-level candidates. If your target job falls in this category, you may wish to adopt a fairly well-established procedure without excessive frills. This chapter is a straightforward guide for writing regular résumés. Follow the guidelines given here and you will turn out perfectly serviceable résumés in a short time.

TIP

However, for a more ambitious résumé, read the author's *Winning Résumé*, also published by Unicorn Books. By combining some of the selling and focusing techniques discussed in the first four chapters of that book with what is given here, entry level candidates can greatly enhance the quality of their résumé while mid- to high-level candidates can put together a masterpiece.

Why Do You Need a Résumé?

The main reason you should have a résumé is simple – most employers request one. And even if the employer does not ask for a résumé, it is easily the most efficient way to present your qualifications, skills and experience to a prospective employer.

TIP

In addition, the résumé writing process itself will help you crystallise your job objective and determine your major skills and achievements. People who write better, more carefully thought-through résumés also perform very much better at the subsequent job interviews! Read about SWOT analysis in Chapter 4 of this book to understand the importance of self-understanding for performing well in interviews.

Which Résumé is Best for You?

There are two basic types of résumé:

- Chronological résumé, usually put in the reverse order, last job first.
- Skills résumé.

Chronological résumé presents your working life experience in a chronological format. This résumé focuses on what you have been doing and what you have achieved. It provides a clear picture of your employment history, focusing on career advancement and gradually increasing job responsibilities.

The skills résumé, on the other hand, focuses on the skills you have acquired while working. It clusters the skills and/or knowledge you have gained under major skill areas. If you have strong job-specific abilities, the skills résumé will showcase it to your advantage.

Select the format that shows your abilities to greater advantage for the job at hand. You may have to write your résumé using both styles. Then read them both objectively. Decide which of the two makes the most of your assets and creates the greater impact. That one is the style for you!

Make Your Résumé Interesting

Most résumés are boring. View your résumé as a marketing document, an effective way to communicate your strengths and achievements. Remember – the employer does not want to hear your life story. He is looking for the best person to do the job. Therefore, convince him that in you he will find the man he seeks. Focus on your achievements. List the facts that support your achievements. Make the reader want to know more!

Appearance and Formatting

Here are a few simple rules. We shall assume that you are using some good word processing software to prepare the final draft of your résumé.

- Do not use fancy font styles! Arial and Times New Roman with font sizes between 10 and 12 are the most appropriate.
- Use bullets. Bullets help structure your résumé. Bullets will also considerably improve the appearance and facilitate easy reading.
- Use white space. A crowded résumé hides the things you want to say.

You may have a conflict between a one-page target and an uncluttered appearance. If so, then appearance should score over the one-page limitation. However, first make sure that all that you have included are vital to sell your candidature. Should you conclude that your case justifies two pages, go ahead.

However, include the vital points of your job-worthiness in the first paragraph of your covering letter and use a powerful 'Objective' statement on the first page of the résumé.

Length

Unless you work in a highly scientific or technical field (four and even more pages are regarded the norm here), we suggest you limit your résumé to one or two pages.

If you must exceed one page, then present key points in the top half of the first page.

Present the Key Points

The résumé is a marketing document, which should only present things that will be to your benefit.

- Use short sentences.
- Drop the "I", say "Achieved 10 per cent increase in sales" rather than "I achieved 10 per cent increase in sales".

A Step-by-step Approach

Here is a step-by-step approach for writing your résumé. When you have worked through the steps below, you will have the raw materials and know-how to construct your résumé. Then, you will need to decide on the type of résumé you wish to use, finally editing and fine-tuning it until it is in a presentable form. You will probably find fine-tuning the hardest part of writing your résumé.

So, let us get to the basics of a résumé. You may read the sections below either in sequence, or jump to the one you wish to learn more about. In each section, you will be introduced to the purpose, shown examples of how the section should look, and offered hints on how to get the job done. The sections are:

- Identifying Information
- The Objective
- Summary of Qualifications
- Education
- Work Experience
- Activities/Interests

Identifying Information

The first section of a résumé is your name, address, phone number, fax and/or e-mail address. You need not actually write the word "résumé" at the top, since it will be obvious to your reader what he is looking at. It is customary to put name, residential address and phone number(s) in this section. It may also be helpful to put your office phone number(s) and perhaps fax and e-mail as well (but only if you may be safely contacted at your present job).

Most correspondence today comes via regular mail or phone but you never know what the future holds! So, add an e-mail address if you have one.

The Objective

The objective is an optional part of the résumé.

Is an Objective Right for You?

Here are some things to consider:

If you know exactly what kind of work you wish to be considered for, then you might want to communicate that in your objective. Defining your purpose for the application is a very good way to start, especially if your application is not in response to an advertised vacancy and, therefore, the reader does not know what type of job you have in mind.

> ***The objective is a general statement of your career goals***

When used, an objective serves the important purpose of telling an employer what position you are seeking. It should convey a sense of clarity in your mind regarding your very next step on the career path. The objective, therefore, should be focused and clearly stated. It should not be a general statement about your life and career goals.

TRAP

The importance of a clear objective statement cannot be over emphasised. In fact, it may be preferable to omit the objective, rather than put something vague. Do not include an empty, fluffy objective. Either draft one that conveys useful information about you, and demonstrates that you know what the employer is looking for, or omit it altogether!

For example, the objective: "To utilise my skills in a challenging position that will afford advancement and professional growth" tells the employer really nothing about you. The statement is too general to be of any value.

Guidelines for Your Objective

If you choose to include an objective, here are some guidelines. An objective may contain up to four parts. However, it is not essential that every objective contain all four. Just include as many parts as are applicable to the job.

Part one is the level of the position. Examples of position levels may be words such as "trainee", "temporary", "part-time", "full-time", "entry level", "experienced", "supervisory" and "executive". If you know what level of position you are seeking, select one of the above terms, or create one of your own. In many cases, position level is not an important part of an objective, and can be left off.

Part two contains the skills you hope to use in that position. Refer to the list of skills given under *Build on Your Strengths* earlier in Chapter 4. This will help you identify the job-relevant skills that you possess. For example, you may be seeking "A position in consulting, software design, development and support utilising my software, customer relations and problem-solving skills".

Part three is the position function, sometimes called position title. If you are responding to a job posting, the position function can often be found in the text of the advertisement. Examples of functions are "chemist", "administrative assistant", "process engineer", "accountant", "project manager", "consultant" etc. For those with broad skill sets, many position titles may apply. Find out what a specific employer calls this function within their organisation from the advertisement or from an acquaintance working in that field. You may also choose to invent a title that is broad enough to encompass your unique vision.

Part four refers to the field or industry in which you hope to work. You need to specify this in job applications that you may send without waiting for a formal job advertisement from a particular industry.

Your particular position may well be found in more than one field or industry. For example, accountants work in all the industries listed above. If your career vision is not focused on any field or industry, then you may wish to omit this part of the objective.

Finally, integrate all four parts into a cohesive whole.

Summary of Qualifications

This part of your résumé is sometimes called an Executive Summary. It can be the most powerful section of your résumé. It is a brief statement of your experience, training and personal abilities. It can be expressed in one short paragraph or in bulleted format. Experts recommend you should limit this to approximately six sentences or bulleted statements.

This part allows you to really talk about yourself in your résumé. It can summarise a breadth of experiences and call attention to skills not represented by your position titles.

It is especially useful when making a career change. Here, you want to immediately call the employer's attention to all the skills you have, not just those that are obvious in your job descriptions.

Writing a summary can be quite a challenge. It requires you to think about your whole work life from a big picture perspective. Many times, people forget what they have done, if it happened some time ago, or have difficulty putting it into words.

TIP

Sometimes, you can jog your memory by looking at a list of action verbs so that you remember things you have done in the past. By searching through a list of verbs, you will not only remember your achievements, but you may also get some ideas for describing your past achievements in new ways. To get a start, you should make a list of what you consider your key skills.

After identifying key skills, you must prepare an appropriate list of verbs. Try writing your summary of qualifications using some of the key skills. Keep in mind your job goal, and think about the key skills necessary to be successful in that area. Now, recalling your career/life experiences, which of those skills have you developed?

The executive summary is also the right place to highlight your relevant personal strengths. While drafting the summary, think of characteristics such as being a team player, being exceptionally organised, being creative, artistic, or detail-oriented.

Think also about the total number of years you have spent in your area of expertise; think about how well rounded your experience is.

While preparing to write your summary of qualifications, a useful trick is to talk aloud about your overall career and job skills and experiences. Be big-picture oriented and summary oriented. An employer can see who you have worked for and can check all the details about your experiences in the rest of your résumé. Now is your chance to help the employer understand how they all fit together.

Sometimes, people find it easier to write this section after they have worked on the rest of their résumé. It is often helpful to go through the details of your skills and experiences, review them closely and then write the Summary of Qualifications at the end.

A summary of qualifications should be written after the entire résumé has been drafted

A close colleague you have worked with for a long time may be a good sounding board when you work on this chapter. Friends who are truly familiar with your work and work style are also good sources of assistance.

Education

This section is designed to show an employer that you have the necessary educational credentials to do the job. Include in this section your traditional degrees and certificates as well as professional courses attended. It should show your academic breadth and intellectual accomplishments. It should even imply something about your industriousness and desire to improve. Continuous learning is essential to remain competitive in today's job world and this section should show what you have done to stay up-to-date in your current field, and how you continue to do so. This section is of key importance if you are making a career change. Here, show how your new or existing academic credentials can be related to the new career you seek.

In addition to higher education degrees and certificates, also include all academic awards or scholarships and professional affiliations you have. Sometimes, it may also benefit you to include your marks obtained and/or rank in class.

Rate Your Résumé

The résumé is a statement about you, written by you. Obviously, a special effort will be needed to make an objective self-assessment! The modest amongst you may be too critical, finding everything wrong with your effort. The less inhibited may get bored and refuse to polish the first draft any further. Both attitudes are counter-productive.

There is need, therefore, to pause now that the first draft is ready. After the first flush of creative energy, there is need for reflection and systematic, objective evaluation so that the rough edges can be smoothed and the entire product can be polished till it shines. The revision is often far more difficult than the drafting itself. You may use the following techniques for an objective self-evaluation. As an additional input, recruit an experienced and trusted friend to critique your résumé if you can.

You be the Judge

The résumé needs to be strong and concise. The objective should clearly state your career goals while the body of the résumé should support the objective logically. Your résumé makes a personal statement about you and your career. It is a written snapshot of your work, education and professional life. It is important that you feel comfortable with your résumé's format and content. If the final product does not make you feel proud to use it as your personal sales tool, take the time to make changes necessary to achieve this goal.

Check your résumé for the following:

1. Overall Appearance
2. Specific Attributes

Under each of these two main factors are several sub-factors. Rate each sub-factor as one of the following:

1. Accept. Give an A.
2. Rework. Give an R.

There is no need to use more gradations such as a scale of 1 to 5. Either the portion under review is okay as it is or it needs more work. There is no middle ground!

The Critique Form

The critique form is in two parts. The first part deals with overall appearance and the second with specific attributes. The first part addresses the structure and appearance of the résumé. The second part evaluates the résumé's actual contents. Evaluate each part on its own merits. That is, do not let contents influence the evaluation of the appearance or appearance influence the evaluation of the contents. Give a break of a day or two between the initial drafting and the critique of your résumé to bring to bear the objectivity you will need.

Multiple Evaluations

If possible, hand out a copy of your draft résumé and a set of evaluation forms to one or two trusted friends.

If you compare their evaluation forms with your own, you will get more than one dependable input to help you edit and polish your masterpiece. Having your friends use structured evaluation forms will yield much more useful information than just a quick overall feedback which may merely say "excellent" or "okay".

Overall Appearance

Appearance Assessment Factors	A	R
Is the layout pleasing to the eye?		
Does the written matter fit comfortably on the page without overcrowding or too much white space?		
Is the résumé on good quality bond paper and the typing clear and unsmudged?		
Is the résumé easily readable? (Bullets used, no long sentences, no obscure fonts, no abbreviations)		

Does the résumé use bold, italics and underlining to highlight strengths?		
Is important information located prominently at the left and near the top of the page whenever possible?		
Overall Rating for Appearance		

Tick the A column for an accept rating and the R column for a reject rating.

Assuming that the résumé passes the appearance test, let us look at it once again from the point of view of the quality of specific attributes.

Specific Attributes

Attribute Rating Factors	A	R
Goal Focused: Does the text support the objective?		
Length: Can it be shortened? Is a page comfortably filled?		
Relevance: Is the material relevant and sequenced in order of importance?		
Format: Is the format (chronological, functional, combination) appropriate for the most favourable presentation?		
Action Orientation: Do sentences and paragraphs begin with action verbs?		
Specificity: Does the résumé avoid generality and focus on specific performance and achievements?		
Completeness: Is all relevant information included?		
Quantified Results: Are the results of your past work experience quantified as far as possible?		
Bottom Line: How well does the résumé accomplish the ultimate purpose of getting the employer to want to interview the applicant?		

If any of the criteria gets a rework rating in any of the two parts, do go through your résumé once again, even if the overall ratings for appearance and/or attributes are acceptable. Pay particular attention to the deficient criterion this time around.

Armed with these two forms, filled in by yourself and one or two trusted friends, you should now have all the inputs you need to produce a masterpiece of a résumé.

TRAP

A word of caution is appropriate here. While we encourage you to get independent evaluations from friends, and to look at these evaluations objectively, it is good to remember that it is your résumé and their advice should be acted on only if you are convinced that by doing so, you will indeed improve on your résumé! So, base your corrective action primarily on your self-evaluation and use the friendly critiques as secondary inputs.

Further Reading

In this section, we have walked you through a complete résumé writing exercise. The thoughts and skills you have learned here should see you through almost any simple résumé writing task that you may encounter.

You must recognise, however, that the product will only be a rough draft. You will have the raw materials assembled, but not the finished product. For mastery over résumé writing, read the author's *Winning Résumé*, also published by Unicorn Books.

For greater insight into body language and the part it plays in reinforcing your positive image, await the author's forthcoming book on this fascinating subject.

Index

Books on Career & Management

275/-

175/-

150/-

296/-

125/-

295/-

96/-

96/-

110/-

info@unicornbooks.in www.unicornbooks.in